ServiceNow IT Operations Management

Demystifying IT Operations Management

Ajaykumar Guggilla

BIRMINGHAM - MUMBAI

ServiceNow IT Operations Management

First published: April 2017

Production reference: 1250417

Published by Packt Publishing Ltd.
Livery Place
35 Livery Street
Birmingham
B3 2PB, UK.
ISBN 978-1-78588-908-0

www.packtpub.com

Credits

Author
Ajaykumar Guggilla

Copy Editors
Dipti Mankame
Safis Editing

Reviewers
Chatarina Lyth
Tcat

Project Coordinator
Judie Jose

Commissioning Editor
Pratik Shah

Proofreader
Safis Editing

Acquisition Editor
Vijin Boricha

Indexer
Pratik Shirodkar

Content Development Editor
Abhishek Jadhav

Graphics
Kirk D'Penha

Technical Editor
Aditya Khadye

Production Coordinator
Shantanu Zagade

Disclaimer

The author has taken the possible measures and made it easy for the reader to use the easily available resources, including most of the steps highlighted in the book that is leveraged using the developer instance, which is available for everyone. You can reset it at `https://developer.servicenow.com/app.do#!/home`. Moreover, for any further clarifications required on the subject, you can navigate to `https://community.servicenow.com/welcome`. Also, the latest documentation and further details are available at the ServiceNow wiki, which has a vast majority of topics covered. Some of the topics or images might have references to ServiceNow wiki. ServiceNow is a trademark of ServiceNow Inc. who owns ServiceNow. The author has no direct involvement with the company. He has just utilized the product capabilities and features to complete the book. The book started the journey during the Geneva release. The author has taken all the measures to update the versions to Helsinki and Istanbul. You might need to refer to ServiceNow wiki for the latest documentation if some of the topics are not clear and you can also get clarification from the ServiceNow community. The author does not warrant that all the instructions mentioned in the book might work the way they are described. All the steps described are based on configurations and settings of various instructions described, for example, IP addresses, attribute information, and other information pertinent to the environment and settings. Furthermore, the author has not utilized any of the external resources either from his employer or other third-party resources. This book was fully written by the author using his own personal developer instance available at ServiceNow.

About the Author

Ajaykumar Guggilla is the holder of a masters in computer applications and is certified in Project Management Professional (PMP), information technology, and Infrastructure Library (ITIL) Expert, Microsoft Certified Professional, PRINCE2, and ServiceNow administrator. Ajay has 19 years of experience in the IT industry. Ajay started his career as a hardcore programmer and evolved to take on many positions at reputable organizations, including Cognizant, PwC, and Sathyam. Ajay has diversified his experience to include IT service delivery, IT infrastructure, enterprise systems, improving quality and maturity, CRM solutions, adopting service management solutions, SAP support, data center migrations, IT Service Management (ITSM)/ITIL, and ServiceNow solutions.

His experience from previous job roles extends to program manager, IT architect, process owner, process lead, director, project manager, engagement manager, process manager, reporting champion, and global production. Ajay has worked with fortune customers in oil and gas, chemicals, automobiles and parts, healthcare, retail, media, travel and leisure, insurance, telecommunications, banks, media and entertainment, insurance, financial services, technology, and intergovernmental organizations.

His knowledge has helped many organizations, including defining the strategy, streamlining the service management process, optimizing the cost, adhering to compliances, increasing the customer satisfaction, process maturity, technology adoption, infrastructure transformation and consolidation, and much more.

Ajay started working with ServiceNow five years back. He has worked on different engagements in helping organizations select their service management tool, has managed ServiceNow programs, has solutioned, architected, and handled end-to-end implementations, and performed process automation and version migrations. He is passionate about working on ServiceNow and loves the product, which has lead him to write this book on ITOM, which will help individuals and organizations improve their operational excellence by implementing ITOM capabilities.

Acknowledgments

Thanks to my parents: my dad, the late Mr. Subramanyam, and my mom, Mrs. Surekha, who gave birth to me, and all the sacrifices they have made to raise me and my siblings. Without them I would not have gained the knowledge I have. Mom and dad, you have been there day after day, to make sure my life turned out this way. I miss you dad. Thanks for the support mom.

An important acknowledgement goes to my sweet and great wife, Mrs. Padma, without whom I would not have completed this book--she has been pushing and motivating me every day throughout the journey to complete this book. She compromised on the family time; at times I feel I have a warrior when she is next to me. Thanks for all your love and motivation my sweet wife.

I can't explain how much my kids missed their dad's time over the course of writing this book. I was lucky to have my sweet kids, Dhrithi and Smrithi, who could understand and be supportive. They used to check with me about the progress of this book. Thanks kids, you are the sweetest.

Thanks to my sisters, Ajitha and Aisu, who supported my growth and education throughout my life by providing guidance and support. Thanks for being my sisters.

My thanks to all my employers: Cognizant, PwC, Event Consulting, and Sathyam, for providing me an opportunity to work at an organization that has, either directly or indirectly, helped me gain the knowledge to write this book.

Thanks to all my colleagues, especially Mr. Raja Rangenathan and Mr. Praveen Challa, my friends, my family, and all others who have helped me either directly or indirectly to complete this book.

Thanks to the Packt team for giving me this opportunity and help in all the stages of completing this book.

Last but not least, I cannot forget to thank Mr. Fred Luddy for creating such a wonderful product, ServiceNow.

About the Reviewers

Chatarina Lyth has 20 years of experience in the IT industry and 10 years of work experience in IT Operations Management. She has, over the years, worked as a consultant, implementing several of the leading ITOM tools in large enterprises, in the private as well as public sectors. Chatarina joined the ServiceNow ITOM team in 2014, and has been part of the journey ServiceNow has made since then.

Tcat (formerly Tim Catura-Houser) transitioned from vacuum-tube (valve) computers in 1965. He got really excited when the Altair got Microsoft BASIC around 1973, because he could have a computer at home. More recently (March 2017), he was surprised with the President's Award from http://www.eta-i.org/ for being a dedicated volunteer.

His career as a global road warrior has included both being a field geek and trainer, only sometimes to his extreme peril. His MCP number 416024 in 2017 marks 20 years as an MCSE.

While some of the titles he has worked on are lost to history, he quit counting after 50. Some of them can be found on Amazon by his former and current names.

> *Certainly, it is easy for me to say I cannot remember doing a tactical editing project that brought me so many smiles. Your author did an amazing job. On the internal side, I experienced equal pleasure. In my own mind I call it the tale of 2 Jays. Judie and Juliana at Packt are two astounding individuals! To me, they are more than professional. They are what I would have to call, buddies.*

www.PacktPub.com

For support files and downloads related to your book, please visit www.PacktPub.com.

Did you know that Packt offers eBook versions of every book published, with PDF and ePub files available? You can upgrade to the eBook version at www.PacktPub.com and as a print book customer, you are entitled to a discount on the eBook copy. Get in touch with us at service@packtpub.com for more details.

At www.PacktPub.com, you can also read a collection of free technical articles, sign up for a range of free newsletters and receive exclusive discounts and offers on Packt books and eBooks.

https://www.packtpub.com/mapt

Get the most in-demand software skills with Mapt. Mapt gives you full access to all Packt books and video courses, as well as industry-leading tools to help you plan your personal development and advance your career.

Why subscribe?

- Fully searchable across every book published by Packt
- Copy and paste, print, and bookmark content
- On demand and accessible via a web browser

Customer Feedback

Thanks for purchasing this Packt book. At Packt, quality is at the heart of our editorial process. To help us improve, please leave us an honest review on this book's Amazon page at https://www.amazon.com/dp/1785889087.

If you'd like to join our team of regular reviewers, you can e-mail us at customerreviews@packtpub.com. We award our regular reviewers with free eBooks and videos in exchange for their valuable feedback. Help us be relentless in improving our products!

Table of Contents

Preface

ServiceNow Information Technology Operations Management (ITOM) teaches you about different applications and plugins that provide different capabilities to reduce disruption caused to the business. The key differentiator between other tools available in the market and ServiceNow ITOM is that the functions are available within ServiceNow to easily leverage the data natively. Each component of the ITOM suite has different capabilities that can be tied to each of the individual components and business services. We can predict outages well in advance and hence take proactive measures to avoid them.

The book's chapters cover the architecture and description of the each of ITOM's components, prerequisites for setting up the capabilites, installation instructions, and then finally explain the important settings and properties.

The book evolved from the Geneva release and has been updated to the Istanbul release. The author has taken all measures to provide improved service availability, immediate visibility of vital business services, and much more, all from the convenience of your single screen.
By the end of this book, you should understand how ServiceNow ITOM functions within the ServiceNow ecosystem.

What this book covers

Chapter 1, *Introduction to IT Operations Management in ServiceNow*, introduces ServiceNow IT Operations Management, the importance of each of ITOM's components, and ITOM's high-level architecture.

Chapter 2, *MID Server Essentials*, walks through all the necessary steps to install MID Server and configure roles.

Chapter 3, *Configuration Management Using ServiceNow Discovery*, covers the different phases available, the ECC queue, and configuring discovery the easy way.

Chapter 4, *Creating and Managing Dependency Views*, focuses on learning the prerequisites, understanding the tables and properties, and learning about how to load and view dependency maps.

Chapter 5, *Cloud Management*, dives further into using cloud functionalities and capabilities, understanding the various out-of-the-box plugins available, understanding the different roles available, and exploring the cloud operational portal. Here, our focus will be on configuring Amazon Cloud Services, and we will touch on how other cloud providers can be configured.

Chapter 6, *Automation Using ServiceNow Orchestration*, discusses orchestration prerequisites and capabilities. Learn about orchestration workflows and run through a real example of using Active Directory objects.

Chapter 7, *Exploring Service Mapping*, discusses the service mapping architecture, what a business service is, how to set up service mapping, and how to perform service mapping using discovery.

Chapter 8, *Monitoring Using Event Management*, deals with event management architecture; setting up the MID Server for event management; exploring event sources and properties; how to configure alert rules, threshold rules, and event transform rules; and exploring the dashboard.

What you need for this book

This book assumes the reader has a good understanding of the Linux operating system, basic knowledge of cloud computing and big data, and some experience with OpenStack software. The book will go through a simple multi-node setup of the OpenStack environment, which may require a basic understanding of networking and virtualization concepts. If you have experience of Hadoop and Spark processes, this is a big plus. Although the book uses VirtualBox, feel free to use any other lab environment, such as a VMware workstation or other tools.

OpenStack can be installed and runs either on bare metal or a virtual machine. However, this book requires that you have enough resources for the whole setup. The minimum hardware or virtual requirements are as follows:

- CPU: 4 cores
- Memory: 8 GB RAM
- Disk space: 80 GB

In this book, you will need the following software:

- Linux Operating System: Centos 7.x
- VirtualBox
- OpenStack RDO distribution, preferably the Liberty release. If you intend to use the Juno or Kilo releases, make sure to change the plugin versions when launching clusters to comply with the correct supported OpenStack version.

Internet connectivity is required to install the necessary OpenStack packages, Sahara images and Sahara image packages for specific plugins.

Who this book is for

To make use of the content of this book, a basic prior knowledge of ServiceNow is expected. If you feel you do not have that knowledge, it is always possible to catch up on the basic requirements by quickly reading up on the major components at the ServiceNow wiki page (`http://wiki.servicenow.com/index.php?title=Main_Page#gsc.tab=0`). This covers the latest updates on ServiceNow Istanbul and future releases. This book provides an overview of the ITOM applications and setting up ITOM's capabilities, using a quick and detailed guided setup. If you currently work with other toolsets, this book also gives you an idea of how ITOM is handled in ServiceNow.

Conventions

In this book, you will find a number of text styles that distinguish between different kinds of information. Here are some examples of these styles and an explanation of their meaning.

Code words in text, database table names, folder names, filenames, file extensions, pathnames, dummy URLs, user input, and Twitter handles are shown as follows: "Credentials are encrypted automatically with a fixed instance key when they are submitted or updated in the credentials (`discovery_credentials`) table."

New terms and **important words** are shown in bold. Words that you see on the screen, for example, in menus or dialog boxes, appear in the text like this: "Now right-click on **Windows** and right-click on **32 bit**, and then download to the server or the local machine where you are going to install the MID Server."

Warnings or important notes appear in a box like this.

 Tips and tricks appear like this.

Reader feedback

Feedback from our readers is always welcome. Let us know what you think about this book-what you liked or disliked. Reader feedback is important for us as it helps us develop titles that you will really get the most out of.

To send us general feedback, simply e-mail `feedback@packtpub.com`, and mention the book's title in the subject of your message.

If there is a topic that you have expertise in and you are interested in either writing or contributing to a book, see our author guide at `www.packtpub.com/authors`.

Customer support

Now that you are the proud owner of a Packt book, we have a number of things to help you to get the most from your purchase.

Downloading the color images of this book

We also provide you with a PDF file that has color images of the screenshots/diagrams used in this book. The color images will help you better understand the changes in the output. You can download this file from `https://www.packtpub.com/sites/default/files/down` `loads/ServiceNowITOperationsManagement_ColorImages.pdf`.

Errata

Although we have taken every care to ensure the accuracy of our content, mistakes do happen. If you find a mistake in one of our books-maybe a mistake in the text or the code-we would be grateful if you could report this to us. By doing so, you can save other readers from frustration and help us improve subsequent versions of this book. If you find any errata, please report them by visiting http://www.packtpub.com/submit-errata, selecting your book, clicking on the **Errata Submission Form** link, and entering the details of your errata. Once your errata are verified, your submission will be accepted and the errata will be uploaded to our website or added to any list of existing errata under the Errata section of that title.

To view the previously submitted errata, go to https://www.packtpub.com/books/content/support and enter the name of the book in the search field. The required information will appear under the **Errata** section.

Piracy

Piracy of copyrighted material on the Internet is an ongoing problem across all media. At Packt, we take the protection of our copyright and licenses very seriously. If you come across any illegal copies of our works in any form on the Internet, please provide us with the location address or website name immediately so that we can pursue a remedy.

Please contact us at copyright@packtpub.com with a link to the suspected pirated material.

We appreciate your help in protecting our authors and our ability to bring you valuable content.

Questions

If you have a problem with any aspect of this book, you can contact us at questions@packtpub.com, and we will do our best to address the problem.

1
Introduction to IT Operations Management in ServiceNow

This chapter is an overview of **IT Operations Management (ITOM)** and it will explain the ServiceNow ITOM capabilities within ServiceNow, which include:

- ServiceNow ITOM overview
- MID Server
- Credentials
- Service mapping
- Dependency views
- Event management
- Orchestration
- Discovery
- Cloud management

ServiceNow IT Operations Management overview

Every organization and business focuses on key strategies, some of them include:

- Time to market
- Agility
- Customer satisfaction
- Return on investment

Information technology is heavily involved in supporting these strategic goals, either directly or indirectly, providing the underlying IT Services with the required IT infrastructure. IT infrastructure includes network, servers, routers, switches, desktops, laptops, and much more. IT supports these infrastructure components enabling the business to achieve its goals. IT continuously supports the IT infrastructure and its components with a set of governance, processes, and tools, which is called *IT Operations Management.*

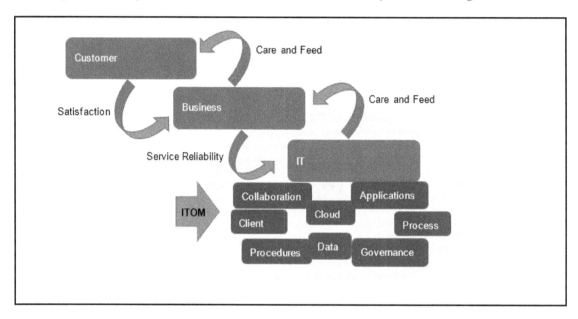

IT cares and feeds the business, and the business expects reliability of services provided by IT to support the underlying business services. A business cares and feeds the customers who expect satisfaction of the services offered to them without service disruption.

Unlike any other tools, it is important to understand the underlying relationship between IT, businesses, and customers. IT just providing the underlying infrastructure and associated components is not going to help; to effectively and efficiently support the business IT needs to understand how the infrastructure, components, and process are aligned and associated with the business services to understand the impact to the business with an associated incident, problem, event, or change that is arising out of an IT infrastructure component.

IT needs to have a consolidated and complete view of the dependency between the business and the customers, not compromising on the technology used, the process followed, the infrastructure components used, which includes the technology used. There needs to be a connected way for IT to understand the relations of these seamless technology components to be able to proactively stop the possible outages before they occur and handle a change in the environment.

On the other hand, a business expects service reliability to be able to support the business services to the customers. There is a huge financial impact of businesses not being able to provide the agreed service levels to their customers. So, there is always a pressure and dependence from the business to IT to provide a reliable service and it does not matter what technology or processes are used.

Customers, as always, expect satisfaction of the services provided by the business, at times these are adversely affected by service outages caused by the IT infrastructure. Customer satisfaction is also a key strategic goal for the business to be able to sustain in the competitive market. IT is also expected to be able to integrate with the customer infrastructure components to provide a holistic view of the IT infrastructure view to effectively support the business by proactively identifying and fixing the outages before they happen, reducing the number of outages and increasing the reliability of IT services delivered.

Most of the tools do not understand the context of the **Service-Oriented Architecture** (**SOA**) connecting the business services to the impacted IT infrastructure components to be able to effectively support the business and also IT to be able to justify the cost and impact of providing end to end service.

Most of the traditional tools perform certain aspects of ITOM functions, some partially and some support integration with the **IT Service Management** (**ITSM**) tool suite. The missing integration piece between the traditional tools and a full blown cloud solution platform is leaning to the SOA.

ServiceNow, a cloud based solution, has focused the lens of true SOA that brings together the ITOM suite providing and leveraging the native data and also connecting to the customer infrastructure to provide a holistic and end-to-end view of the IT Service at a given snapshot.

With ServiceNow IT has a complete view of the business service and technical dependencies in real time leveraging powerful individual capabilities, applications, and plugins within ServiceNow ITOM.

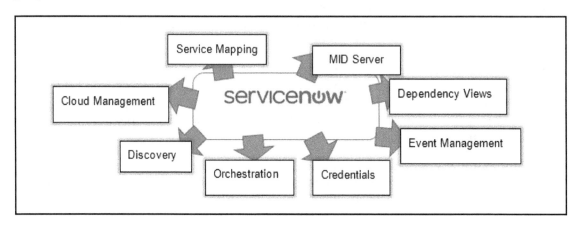

ServiceNow ITOM comprises the ServiceNow application and plugins. Not all the applications and plug-ins come out-of-the-box, some of the plugins, and applications have license restrictions that require separate licensing or subscriptions to be purchased. More detailed information is given in the subsequent chapters. The following are different components of plug-ins and applications and that make up ServiceNow IT Operations Management.

- **Management, Instrumentation, and Discovery (MID) Server**: The MID Server helps to establish communication and data movement between ServiceNow and the external corporate network and application
- **Credentials**: This is a platform that stores credentials including usernames, passwords, or certificates in an encrypted field on the credentials table that is leveraged by ServiceNow discovery
- **Service mapping**: Service mapping discovers and maps the relationships between IT components that comprise specific business services, even in dynamic, virtualized environments
- **Dependency views**: Dependency views graphically display an infrastructure view with relationships of configuration items and the underlying business services
- **Event management**: Event management provides a holistic view of all the events that are triggered from various event monitoring tools
- **Orchestration**: Orchestration helps in automating IT and business processes for operations management

- **Discovery**: Works with MID Server and explores the IT infrastructure environment to discover the configuration items and populating the **Configuration Management Database (CMDB)**
- **Cloud management**: Helps to easily manage third-party cloud providers, which include AWS, Microsoft Azure, and VMware clouds

Understanding ServiceNow IT Operations Management components

Now that we have covered what ITOM is about and focused on ServiceNow ITOM capabilities, let's deep dive and explore more about each capability.

Dependency views

In this section, we will near about the importance of dependency views.

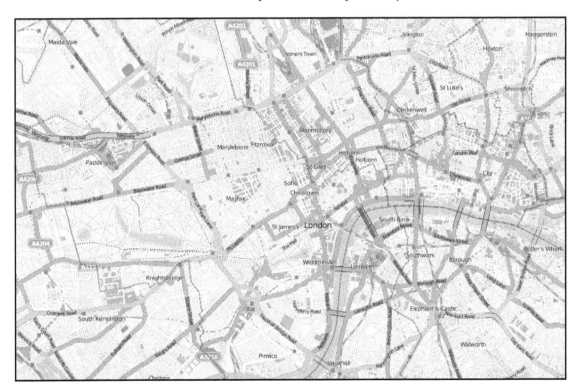

Maps like the preceding one are becoming so important in everyday life; imagine a world without GPS devices or electronic maps.

There are also hard copies of the maps that were available everywhere for us to get from place to place. There are also special maps to the utilities and other public service agencies to be able to identify the impact of digging a tunnel or a water pipe or an underground electric cable. These maps help them to identify the impact of making a change to the ground.

Maps also helps us to understand the relationships between states, countries, cities, and streets with different set of information in real time that includes real-time traffic information showing accident information, any constructions, and so on.

Dependency views is similar to real life navigation maps; they provide a map of relationships between the IT Infrastructure components and the business services that are defined under the scope. Unlike the real-time traffic updates on the maps the dependency views show real-time active incidents, change, and problems reported on an individual configuration item or an infrastructure component.

Changes frequently happen in the environment. Some of the changes are handled with a legacy knowledge of how the individual components are connected to the business services through the service mapping plugin down to the individual component level. Making a change without understanding the relationships between each IT infrastructure component might adversely affect the service levels and impact the business service.

ServiceNow dependency views provide a snapshot of how the underlying business service is connected to individual **Configuration Item** (**CI**) elements. A configuration item is referred to as tangible or intangible infrastructure component or an element that might include Infrastructure components, process, procedures etc. Drilling down to the individual CI elements provides a view of associated service operations and service transition data that includes incidents logged against a given CI, any underlying problem reported against the given CI, and also changes associated with the given CI.

Dependency views provides a graphical view of configuration items and their relationships. The dependency views provide a view of the CI and their relationships; in order to get a perspective from a business stand point you will need to enable the service mapping plugin.

Having a detailed view of how the individual CI components are connected from the Business service to the CI components compliments change management, making it possible to perform effective impact analysis before any changes are made to the respective CI:

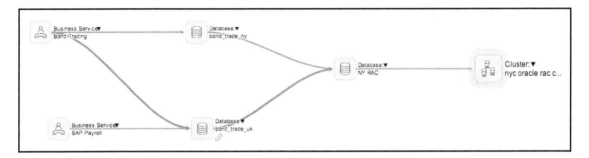

Image source: wiki.ServiceNow.com

A dependency map starts with a root node, which is usually termed as a root CI that is grayed out with a gray frame. Relationships start building up and they map from the upstream and downstream dependencies of the infrastructure components that are scoped to discover by the ServiceNow auto discovery. Administrators have control of the number of levels displayed the dependency maps.

It is also easy to manage maps that allow creating or modifying existing relationships right from the map that posts the respective changes to the CMDB automatically.

Each of the CI component of the dependency maps has an indicator that shows any active and pending issues against a CI; this includes any incidents, problems, changes, and any events associated with the respective configuration item.

Dependency maps can also be created manually by creating CI and creating relationships between them to create dependency maps.

Cloud management

In the earlier versions prior to ServiceNow, there was no direct way to manage cloud instances, people had to create orchestration scripts to manage the cloud instances and also create custom roles.

Managing and provisioning has become easy with the ServiceNow cloud management application. The cloud management application seamlessly integrates with the ServiceNow service catalog. A Service Catalog provides a catalogs of services offered by an organization which has workflows built in with automation capability using orchestration workflows. The cloud management application fully integrates the life cycle management of virtual resources into standard ServiceNow data collection, management, analytics, and reporting capabilities.

The ServiceNow cloud management application provides easy and quick options to key private cloud providers, which include:

- **AWS Cloud**: Manages **Amazon Web Services** (**AWS**) using AWS Cloud
- **Microsoft Azure Cloud**: The Microsoft Azure Cloud application integrates with Azure through the service catalog and provides the ability to manage virtual resources easily
- **VMware Cloud**: The VMware Cloud application integrates with VMware vCenter to manage virtual resources by integrating with the service catalog

The following figure describes a high-level architecture of the cloud management application:

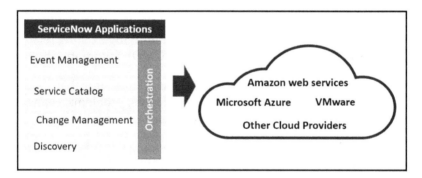

Key features with the cloud management applications include the following:

- A single pane of glass to manage the virtual services in public and private cloud environment including approvals, notifications, security, asset management, and so on
- The ability to repurpose configurations through resource templates that help to reuse the capability sets

- Seamless integration with the service catalog, with a defined workflow and approvals integration, can be done end to end right from the user request to the cloud provisioning
- The ability to control the leased resources through date controls and role-based security access
- The ability to use the ServiceNow discovery application to discover the infrastructure components or the standalone capability to discover virtual resources and their relationships in their environments
- The ability to control and manage virtual resources effectively with a controlled termination shutdown date
- The ability to perform a price calculation and integration of managed virtual machines with asset management
- The ability to automatically or manually provision the required cloud environment with zero click options

There are different roles within the cloud management applications, here are some of them:

- **Virtual provisioning cloud administrator**: The administrator owns the cloud admin portal and end-to-end management including configuration of the cloud providers. They have access to be able to configure the service catalog items that will be used by the requesters and the approvals required to provision the cloud environment.
- **Virtual provisioning cloud approver**: Who either approves or rejects requests for virtual resources.
- **Virtual provisioning cloud operator**: The operator fulfills the requests to manage the virtual resources and the respective cloud management providers. Cloud operators are mostly involved when a manual human intervention is required to manage or provision the virtual resources.

- **Virtual provisioning cloud user**: Users have access to the my virtual assets portal that helps them to manage the virtual resources they own, have requested, or are responsible for.

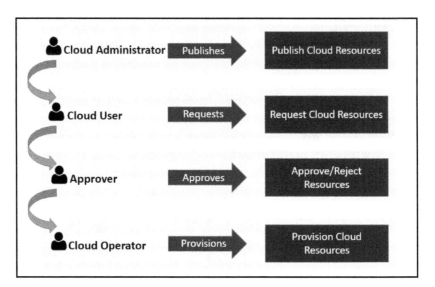

How clouds are provisioned

- The cloud administrator creates a service catalog item for users to be able to request for cloud resources
- The cloud user requests for a virtual machine through the service catalog
- The request goes to the approver who either approves or rejects it
- The cloud operator provisions the requests manually or virtual resources are auto provisioned

Discovery

Imagine how an atlas is mapped and how places have been discovered using exploration devices including manually, by satellite, by survey maps, or by street maps collector devices.

These devices crawl through all the streets to collect different data points that include information about the streets, houses, and much more.

This information is used by consumers for various purposes, including GPS devices, finding and exploring different areas, finding the address of a location, checking for any incidents, constructions, or road closures on the way, and so on.

ServiceNow discovery works in the same way, ServiceNow discovery explores the enterprise network, identifying the devices in scope. ServiceNow discovery probes and sensors perform the collection of infrastructure devices connected to a given enterprise network. Discovery uses probes to determine which TCP ports are opened and to see if it responds to the SNMP queries and sensors to explore any given computer or device, starting first with basic probes and then using more specific probes as it learns more.

Discovery explores to check on the type of device, for each type of device, discovery uses different kinds of probes to extract more information about the computer or device, and the software that is running on it.

CMDB is populated through ServiceNow discovery. ServiceNow discovery searches for devices on the network, when ServiceNow discovery finds a device match within the CMDB; either CMDB gets updated with an existing CI or a new CI is created within the CMDB. Discovery can be scheduled to perform the scan at certain intervals; configuration management keeps the up-to-date status of the CI through discovery.

During discovery, the MID Server looks back on the probes to run from the ServiceNow instance and executes probes to retrieves the results to the CMDB with in the ServiceNow instance. No data is retained on the MID Server. The data collected by these probes is processed by sensors.

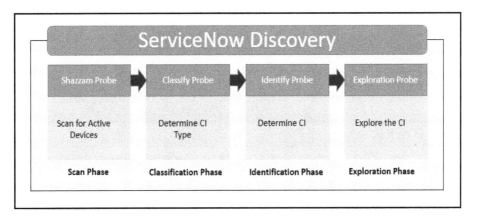

Discovery architecture

ServiceNow is hosted in ServiceNow data centers spanned across the globe. ServiceNow as an application does not have the ability to communicate with any given enterprise network. Traditionally, there are two different types of discovery tool on the market:

- **Agent based**: An agent is a piece of software installed on the servers or individual systems that sends all information about the system to the CMDB.
- **Agentless**: Agentless discovery doesn't require any individual installations on the systems or components. They utilize a single system or piece of software to probe and sense the network by scanning and federating the CMDB.

ServiceNow is an agentless discovery that does not require any individual software to be installed, but it does require MID Server to be installed on the network where discovery has to be run. Discovery is available as a separate subscription from the rest of the ServiceNow platform and requires the discovery plugin.

MID Server is Java software that runs on any windows or UNIX or Linux system that resides within the enterprise network that needs to be discovered. MID Server is the bridge and communicator between the ServiceNow instance that is sitting somewhere on the cloud and the enterprise network that is secured and controlled.

MID Server uses several techniques to probe devices without using agents. Depending on the type of infrastructure components, MID Server uses the appropriate protocol to gather information from the infrastructure component. For example, to gather information from network devices MID Server will use **Simple Network Management Protocol** (**SNMP**), to connect to the Unix systems MID Server will use SSH.

The following table shows different ServiceNow discovery probe types:

Device	Probe type
Windows computers and servers	Remote WMI queries, shell commands
UNIX and Linux servers	Shell command (via SSH protocol)
Storage	CIM/WBEM queries
Printers	SNMP queries
Network gear (switches, routers, and so on)	SNMP queries
Web servers	HTTP header examination
Uninterruptible Power Supplies (**UPS**)	SNMP queries

Credentials

ServiceNow discovery and orchestration features require credentials to be able to access the enterprise network; these credentials vary depending on network and device. Credentials such as usernames, passwords, and certificates need a secure place to store these credentials.

ServiceNow credentials applications store credentials in an encrypted format on a specific table within the credentials table.

Credential tagging allows workflow creators to assign individual credentials to any activity in an orchestration workflow or assign different credentials to each occurrence of the same activity type in an orchestration workflow. Credential tagging also works with credential affinities. Credentials can be assigned an order value that forces the discovery and orchestration to try all the credentials when orchestration attempts to run a command or discovery tries to query.

Credentials tables contain many credentials, based on pattern of usage the credential applications knows which credential to use for a faster logon to the device next time.

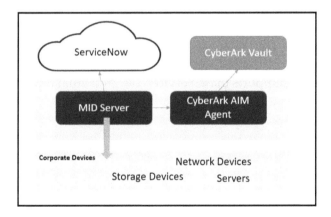

Credentials are encrypted automatically with a fixed instance key when they are submitted or updated in the credentials (`discovery_credentials`) table. When credentials are requested by the MID Server, the platform decrypts the credentials using the following process:

1. The credentials are decrypted on the instance with the fixed key.
2. The credentials are re-encrypted on the instance with the MID Server's public key.

3. The credentials are encrypted on the load balancer with SSL.
4. The credentials are decrypted on the MID Server with SSL.
5. The credentials are decrypted on the MID Server with the MID Server's private key.

A ServiceNow instance can store credentials used by discovery, orchestration, and service mapping in an external credential repository rather than directly in a ServiceNow credentials record.

Currently, the ServiceNow platform supports the use of the CyberArk vault for external credential storage

The ServiceNow credential application integrates with the **CyberArk** credential storage. The MID Server integration with CyberArk vault enables orchestration and discovery to run without storing any credentials on the ServiceNow instance.

The instance maintains a unique identifier for each credential, the credential type (such as SSH, SNMP, or Windows), and any credential affinities. The MID Server obtains the credential identifier and IP address from the instance, and then uses the CyberArk vault to resolve these elements into a usable credential.

The CyberArk integration requires the external credential storage plugin, which is available by request.

The CyberArk integration supports these ServiceNow credential types:

- CIM
- JMS
- SNMP community
- SSH
- SSH private key (with key only)
- VMware
- Windows

Orchestration activities that use these network protocols support the use of credentials stored on a CyberArk vault:

- SSH
- PowerShell
- JMS
- SFTP

MID Server

The Internet has become a prime utility for our day-to-day survival. The availability of Wi-Fi or hard cable network is provided by Internet service providers, these cables run through several miles across different cities, states, and countries. To subscribe to Internet services, our provider places a modem in our home. This modem allows the service provider to enable the Internet capabilities in your home and to link to their network and control them.

Similarly, ServiceNow is a cloud-based application and there are many customers who subscribe and use ServiceNow. ServiceNow is like the Internet service provider, instead of a modem there is something called *MID Server* that needs to be configured for ServiceNow to be able to communicate with the enterprise network. A piece of software needs to run on the enterprise network and be configured for ServiceNow to be able to communicate with the MID Server and be able to talk to the infrastructure components.

The MID Server facilitates communication and movement of data between the ServiceNow platform and external applications, data sources, and services. MID Server is a simple Java application that can run on Windows, Linux, or Unix environments; it facilitates the data exchange between the enterprise network and ServiceNow instance. As MID Server communications are initiated inside the enterprise firewall, they do not require any special firewall rules.

MID Server is not only used by discovery, but it is used by various other components within ServiceNow, which include:

- Discovery
- Orchestration
- Import sets
- Altiris
- Microsoft SMS/SCCM

- Avocent LANDesk
- HP OpenView Operations
- Microsoft **System Center Operations Manager (SCOM)**
- Borland Starteam Integration
- Microsoft MIIS
- Service assurance

The following figure shows the high level architecture of the MID Server and interaction points:

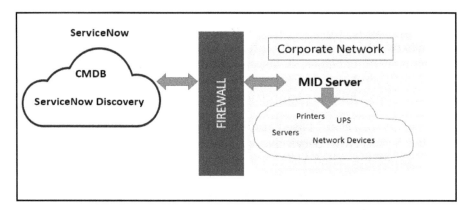

The ECC queue is a connection point between an instance and other systems.

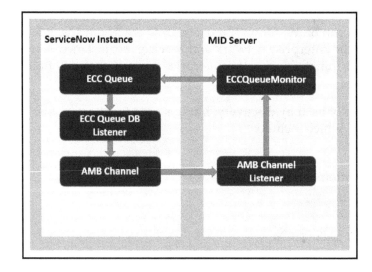

The MID Server subscribes to messages published by the **Asynchronous Message Bus (AMB)**, which notifies the MID Server about waiting jobs assigned to it. The MID Server opens a persistent connection to the instance through the AMB and listens on the /mid/server/<mid_sys_id> AMB channel. When an output record is inserted into the queue (ecc_queue) table, an AMB message is sent to the MID Server's channel. The MID Server receives this message and immediately polls the ecc_queue table for work:

- If a job exists in the ECC queue for that MID Server , the MID Server sets the status to *I'm working on it*
- It then does the work that is requested
- Then it reports the findings of the job back to the ECC queue

Depending on infrastructure factors that include the size of infrastructure there might be a need to place multiple MID Servers in the enterprise network. Placing multiple MID Servers will reduce the load and distribute the functionality between the MID Servers and what they are intended for. For example, there might be five MID Servers that are being used for only SSO integration and there might be an MID Server used for orchestration.

MID Server can be installed on a single machine or multiple MID Servers on a single machine.

There are several factors that need to be considered to determine if multiple MID Servers are required:

- **Network**: In a WAN deployment, deploying and having one MID Server to probe the WAN network might be a huge load and might impact the performance of the MID Server, the best way is to deploy MID Server into a different LAN network
- **Security**: Security policy controlled network devices with Access **Control List (ACL)** might require additional MID Servers on a machine in the network that is already on the ACL
- **Capacity and response time**: When the volume of configuration items to be discovered are high, multiple MID Servers need to be installed for it to be able to return responses quickly
- **Probes**: Depending on the type of probe there might be a need for separate MID Servers for each type of probe

MID Servers are placed at the lowest domain level in a domain separated environment.

Orchestration

Imagine a world where a data center is situated several miles away from a corporate office, even rebooting the server requires a big commute to the data center. Imagine desktop technicians going through each desktop and installing software on each system. Imagine several manual steps in provisioning an AD or a virtual resource. Things have changed and people expect a speedy service and a more automated way of removing manual steps.

Orchestration is the automated arrangement, coordination, and management of complex computer systems, middleware, and services. Thanks to the automation tools available, it makes things much simpler. ServiceNow orchestration capabilities, unlike any other tools, provide orchestration or automation capabilities. Orchestration automates simple or complex multi-system tasks on remote services, servers, applications, and hardware. Orchestration is available as a separate subscription from the rest of the ServiceNow platform.

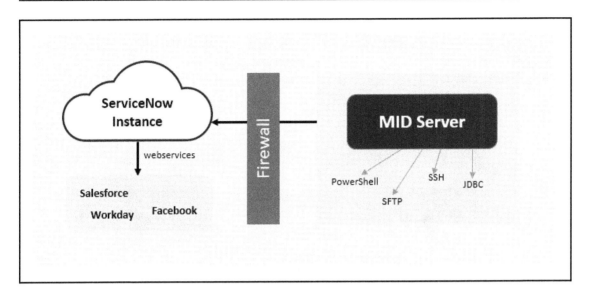

Orchestration provides the ability to make calls outside of a ServiceNow instance, directly to SOAP and REST web services, or to systems within an enterprise's corporate firewall through the MID Server. ServiceNow has workflow editor to create and define workflows across the different applications. The Orchestration extends the workflow editor by providing these features:

Activity packs containing ready-to-use activities:

- An activity designer that allows developers to create custom activities without having to rely on scripting
- The ability to create activity packs using scoped applications
- A databus for reusable data

When an orchestration activity starts within a workflow, orchestration launches a probe and writes a probe record to the ECC queue. The workflow pauses as the MID Server picks up the request and executes the probe. When the probe reports back, the workflow resumes as the results are analyzed. The workflow can exit or continue at this point.

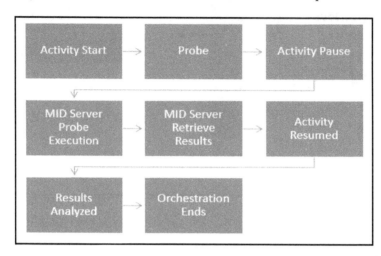

Orchestration extends the ServiceNow workflow to interact with systems outside the ServiceNow instance. Orchestration provides custom activity packs you can use to automate tasks such as employee onboarding, user access rights, server management, and managed file transfers.

MID Server plays an important role in providing orchestration capability. MID Servers are associated with IP address ranges, enabling orchestration to select the correct MID Server to use for an orchestration activity based on the IP address of the target machine.

This functionality ensures that an MID Server with proper privileges is available wherever orchestration probes need to operate in a network. Auto finder also enables administrators to define specific capabilities for each MID Server within an IP address range.

Some of the automation that ServiceNow orchestration can perform includes the following VMware (through vCenter):

- Amazon EC2 instances
- Any system presenting web services
- Windows **Active Directory (AD)**
- Microsoft Exchange mail servers
- Puppet labs Puppet (with configuration automation)
- Chef (with configuration automation)
- Any system accessible from the command line

The AD activity pack enables an administrator to create, delete, and manage objects in Windows AD, such as users, groups, and computers, using a ServiceNow orchestration workflow.

For example, you can reset a password automatically from a user request. You can manage any user account in AD with these activities, whether or not it was created by an orchestration workflow. Orchestration workflow can perform the following in relation to the Activity directory:

- Add a user to group AD activity
- Change an AD user password
- Create an AD object
- Disable an AD user account
- Enable an AD user account
- Check if an AD account is locked
- Query AD
- Remove an AD object
- Remove a user from group AD activity
- Reset an AD user password
- Unlock an AD account
- Update an AD object

Orchestration provides several applications with your subscription:

- **Orchestration ROI**: The orchestration ROI application computes savings resulting from automated tasks in your instance, based on the hourly rate selected for performing tasks manually and the time period of the evaluation. Orchestration ROI estimates your savings by multiplying the cost of performing repetitive tasks manually by the estimated number of times the system performs those tasks automatically during a specific date/time range. The system also calculates the actual savings of your automations. Orchestration ROI is included with the base orchestration subscription. Orchestration ROI reports offer a number of views of the comparative data and allow you to access the associated records directly from the reports.

- **Client software distribution**: The **Client Software Distribution** (**CSD**) application allows administrators to distribute software from the service catalog using third-party management systems. CSD allows an administrator to create all the records necessary to deploy software from service catalog requests, including software models and catalog items. CSD also integrates with software asset management to track license counts for deployed software. Deployment is accomplished using orchestration activities and workflows.

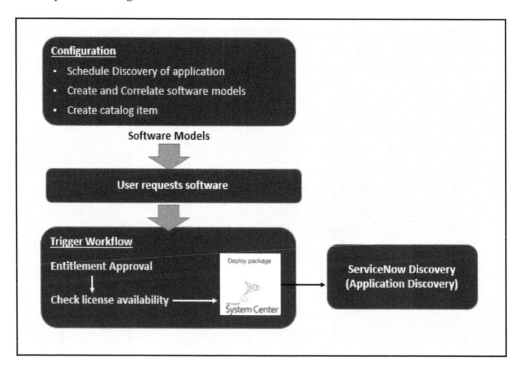

- **Configuration automation**: Configuration automation allows you to use ServiceNow orchestration, Puppet, and Chef to provision and configure individual servers or groups of servers in your network. Chef is a server management application that can use ServiceNow CI data to bring Linux or Windows computers into a desired state by managing files, services, or packages installed on physical or virtual machines. Puppet is a server management application that can use CMDB data to bring computers into a desired state by managing files, services, or packages installed on physical or virtual machines. The ServiceNow application can interact with Puppet systems that run on Linux.
- **Password reset and password change**: The password reset application allows end users to use a self-service process to reset their own passwords on the local ServiceNow instance. Alternatively, your organization can implement a process that requires service-desk personnel to reset passwords for end users. The password change application extends the password reset application by letting admins define how users change their passwords.
- **Self-service process**: Users reset their password over the Internet using a browser on all supported interfaces, including mobile devices.
- **Service-desk password reset process**: Users reset their passwords with the assistance of a service-desk employee, over the phone or in person.

Service mapping

The organization provides services to its customers. IT plays a critical role in providing services to the business community who actually deliver the services to the end users or sell the products. Each line of a separate product line or type of service provided is called a **business service**. Some examples of business services include:

- Financial institutions such as a bank might have business services such as loans, credit cards, banking accounts, and so on
- In a health care pharmacy business, services might include research, development, and manufacturing
- In an oil and gas business, services might be downstream, upstream, manufacturing, research and development, and shipping

Each organization has exclusive types of business services to offer, some of the business services might overlap, which are pertinent to the same type of domain. A business service view to IT is most important to understand how IT is impacting the business or supporting a business service. Service mapping helps to bridge the gap to understand how IT is connected to the business. Service mapping helps to build a detailed map of all the configuration items, including all the hardware and software related configuration items used in a business service.

In some of the organizations people usually take an inventory of the list of configuration items that are isolated individually. These do not have any view of how configuration items are connected to a given business service, these types of mapping are called horizontal mapping, which just has relation to how CI's are connected to individual configuration item components, but no relation to each component of the configuration item. In a service mapping there is a holistic view of how different CI's components are mapped to other individual components of a business service.

Service mapping collects data about devices and applications used in business services in the organization. It then creates a map of business services and writes the collected data into the CMDB. Service mapping uses patterns to discover and map CIs. A typical service mapping pattern consists of two types of algorithms--one for CI identification and one for finding CI connections.

Business service maps show the snapshot of the interconnection between the infrastructure and the business service, service mapping helps to regenerate the maps with up-to-date information.

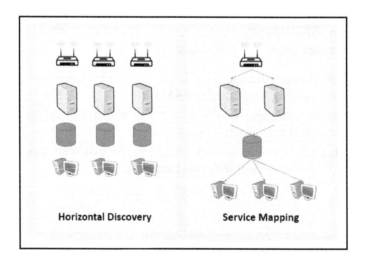

Horizontal Discovery   **Service Mapping**

Service mapping creates maps of the business services by working together with other ServiceNow components. Service mapping uses the ECC queue and MID Servers for discovery and it writes discovered information into CMDB.

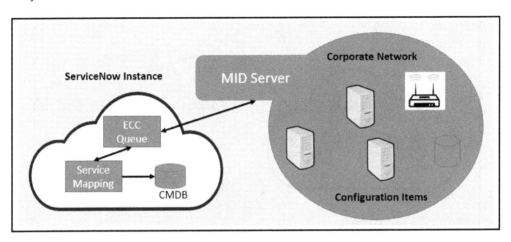

Mapping of devices is dependent on how the MID Server is set up and how discovery is configured. There might be a need of multiple MID Servers based on several factors, including configuration items sitting on a dematerialized zone and also secured network, multiple MID Servers are placed to discover data from multiple sources, and doing the service mapping.

The following figure describes how MID Server is set up in a domain separation environment:

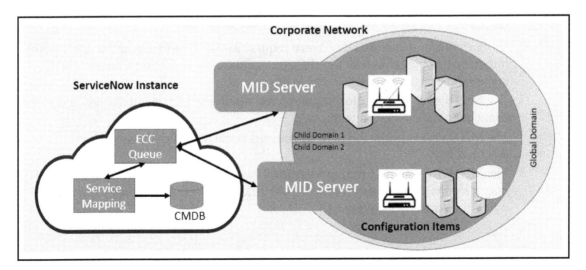

How service mapping works

In this section, lets explore and see how Service Mapping works.

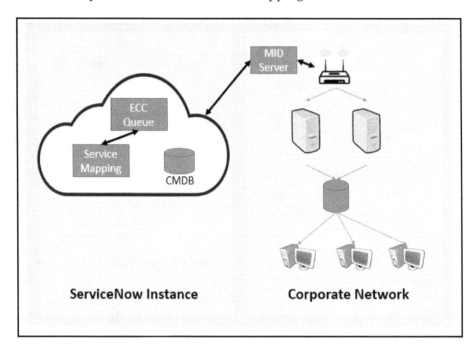

1. For every discovery request, service mapping selects MID Server, by default service mapping selects the MID Server whose IP ranges matches the IP in the discovery request. If there is not a match service mapping selects the default MID Server.
2. Service mapping creates a discovery request for the IP address of the entry point. It then writes the request in the (**ECC**External Communication Channel (ECC) queue and assigns an MID Server to the request.
3. The MID Server passes information on the discovered CI, its attributes, and connections to the ECC queue.
4. The MID Server checks the ECC queue and retrieves the discovery request assigned to it.
5. The MID Server starts running identification sections of the pattern to find the match for the entry point. When the identification section matches the entry point, the pattern discovers a CI.

6. The MID Server starts running connectivity sections of the pattern to find outgoing connections of the newly discovered CI.
7. Service mapping checks the ECC queue and receives information on the newly discovered CI.
8. Service mapping writes the information into the CMDB and adds this CI to the business service map.

Event management

Incidents occur in the IT Infrastructure that impacts a business service. These incidents originate from various sources, such as events and alerts. The IT infrastructure is monitored by various different sets of monitoring tools at different organizations. These monitoring tools collect data from the individual infrastructure components about their activity and signs of abnormality, these might be log messages, warnings, errors, failure messages, security messages, and so on. These messages are called events. ServiceNow event management helps to identify issues across the infrastructure in a single pane of glass or management console by providing event and alert analysis to ensure service availability with the ability to:

- Configure rules for triggering incidents and remediation actions
- Configure alert binding to CIs, services, and hosts for root cause analysis
- Track events from various systems on a single console
- Monitor the alerts console for real-time event processing
- Review the color-coded service maps to see high priority alerts and events
- Use dashboards for monitoring, analysis, and remediation of alerts
- Get a history of previous alerts and events
- Review impact relationships between parent and child CIs
- Review impact and severity calculations based on alerts to prioritize work
- Remediate alerts by integrating with orchestration

An alert is a notification generated by event management for selected events that are considered to be important and require attention. As part of the alert life cycle, you can manage alerts in the following ways:

- Acknowledge alerts
- Create a task such as an incident, problem, or change
- If automatic remediation tasks apply to the alert, begin automatic remediation to start a workflow

- Complete all tasks or remediation activities
- Close alerts for resolved issues
- Add additional information, such as a knowledge article for future reference

The generation of alerts is based on event rules. Event management processes events, generates alerts, and manages alert and incident resolution. Event management either pulls events from supported external event sources using an MID Server.

Event management leverages service mapping data and also data from service analytics to resolve an alert that is raised from the IT infrastructure component. Events are related to the configuration items in the CMDB; when an event is generated, event management locates the associated CI for generating an alert.

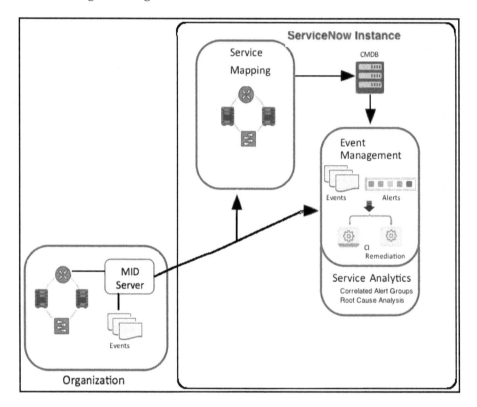

Source: wiki.servicenow.com

Event rules can be configured in ServiceNow with the ability to perform and take certain actions as required. Detailed event information associated with individual events or a group of eventent information associated with individual events or a group of events with individual rules set can be viewed within ServiceNow.

If an event rule or event field mapping used the event or group of events to generate an alert, the event information appears in the Activity section of the alert. Event management within ServiceNow has the ability to manage external events and also configure alerts for discovered business services.

Event management workflow

High-level workflow of event management in ServiceNow is described in the following list:

- Events from other monitoring tools that are integrated and fed into ServiceNow are stored in the event table, which is the `em_event` table first.
- Events are then processed for appropriate escalation by referring to the CMDB. For example, some of the events raised by critical business service and associated infrastructure might be resolved as a critical event and they follow the appropriate escalation rules that are configured.
- Unintended events are filtered out at the next state.
- Alert tables are referenced next for taking appropriate actions against the raised and processed events.
- During events processing the correlation is done this point by either overwriting or preventing recursion alerts.
- Appropriate remediation tasks are created at the next state. At places where automated self-healing solutions are in place, orchestration tasks kick in according to the configured parameters.

- Tasks and remediation related activities utilize the task and the remediation table.

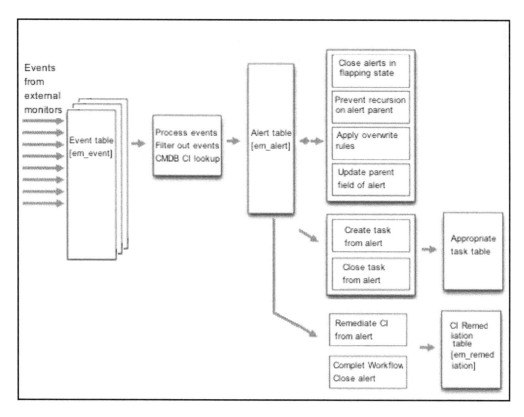

Source : wiki.servicenow.com

Summary

In this chapter, we covered an overview of ITOM, explored different ServiceNow ITOM components including high-level architecture, functional aspects of ServiceNow ITOM components that include service mapping, discovery, event management, MID Server, credentials, service mapping, dependency views, orchestration, discovery, and cloud management.

In the next chapter, we will start detailing each of the individual ITOM components, especially the MID Server. We will describe prerequisites, any license requirements, and also how to set up and configure the individual ITOM component.

2
MID Server Essentials

MID Server is one of the important components in ServiceNow. MID Server is a piece of software installed on a computer at a given network. In this chapter, we will learn about how the MID Server works, MID Server installation, and MID Server configuration steps.

MID Server architecture

In `Chapter 1`, *Introduction to IT Operations Management in ServiceNow*, we covered the architecture of an MID Server. In this chapter, we will explore how to set up an MID Server in technical detail and the prerequisites needed.

Summarizing what we learnt about MID Server, ServiceNow is a SaaS-based application that requires some form of communication mechanism to be able to talk to corporate networks. MID Server plays an important role within ServiceNow as it helps various applications within the ServiceNow suite to facilitate data exchange and establish communications between ServiceNow instances and corporate networks.

MID Server is an important plugin within ServiceNow that is utilized by various applications within ServiceNow, not limited to the following various integrations:

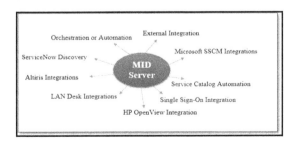

Applications that leverage MID Server

MID Server is Java software that is installed on a compatible server within the corporate network, this makes the communication secure enough to talk to the corporate network by not exposing any security drawbacks. Depending on the type of infrastructure set up, multiple MID Servers are placed within the network. MID Server is installed behind the company firewall, allowing communication between ServiceNow and the rest of the company network.

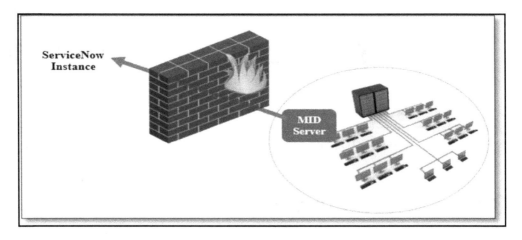

MID Server setup

MID Server communications

MID Server communications happen through an **External Communications Channel** (**ECC**) queue. One way to think about the ECC queue is like an airline check-in kiosk. MID Servers check each of these kiosks on a regular basis to see if there are any activities that need to be performed. If there is any activity then MID Server does the job and sends the information back to the ECC queue, which is utilized by the ServiceNow instance to use. ECC queue is an integration point between other systems and the ServiceNow instance. ECC queue is a table in the ServiceNow database that stores messages that are entered through other systems. Messages are classified as output and input messages:

- **Output messages**: Messages from the ServiceNow instance to some other system
- **Input messages**: Messages from other systems to the ServiceNow instance

The MID Server subscribes to messages published by the **Asynchronous Message Bus** (**AMB**), which notifies the MID Server that it has pending tasks in the ECC queue.

The MID Server opens a persistent connection to the instance through the AMB and listens on the /mid/server/<mid_sys_id | AMB channel. When an output record is inserted into the queue [ecc_queue] table, an AMB message is sent to the MID Server's channel. The MID Server receives this message and immediately polls the ecc_queue table for work.

 The MID Server polls the ECC queue on the regular intervals defined in the mid.poll.time configuration parameter, regardless of AMB message activity. The default polling interval is set to 40 seconds, but it can be reconfigured. This polling of the ECC queue at a regular interval is done in case the AMB connection is dropped.

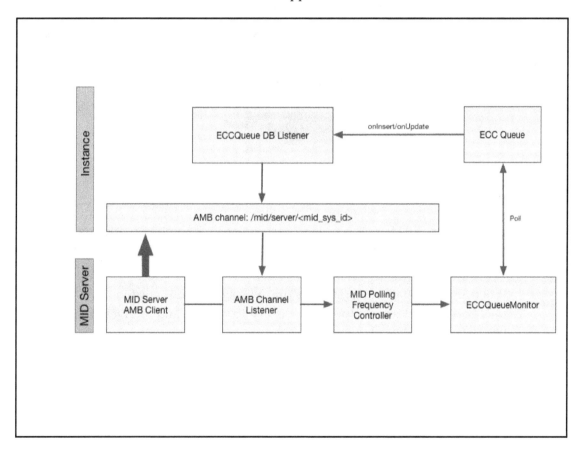

Source: wiki.servicenow.com

MID Server use case in an orchestration workflow

In the following figure, we can see how an MID Server is utilized in an orchestration workflow:

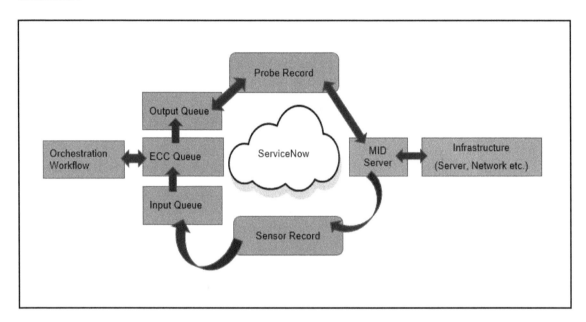

In the preceding figure, MID Server is used to perform an orchestration workflow. The following steps show how the communication happens from the ECC queue to the MID Server and back to the orchestration workflow:

1. When an orchestration workflow is run, a probe record is created
2. MID Server checks the output queue every 15 seconds and receives the probe record from the output queue.
3. MID Server finds the probe record and it reads through and executes against the specified target system or infrastructure component.
4. MID Server now returns the response back of the payload from the probe into the input queue.
5. Orchestration workflow looks at the output queue on the response back from the MID Server and follows the rest of the defined orchestration steps or scripts that need to be executed.

MID Server, which is placed in the corporate networks, queries every 15 seconds to search for probe records. These parameters of 15 seconds frequencies can be adjusted to avoid unnecessary traffic in a multiple MID Server deployment scenario.

Once the probe records are executed, the results are posted back to the ServiceNow instance. Sensors are processors of the probe records, sensors decide how to precede on communicating with the particular infrastructure component. MID Server makes only outbound calls with no inbound calls made from ServiceNow to the MID Server. MID Server communications are securely initiated through SOAP on the HTTPS (port 443) within the enterprise firewall.

Unlike how different people talk different languages to communicate, MID Server uses different probe technologies to communicate with different types of infrastructure components, some of them include PowerShell, SSH, and so on.

MID Server prerequisites

In this section, we will cover the detailed prerequisites required to set up MID Server including any license requirements.

- **Required ServiceNow plugins**:
    - MID Server
- **External dependency**: Ability to access networks without any restriction
- **System requirements**:
    - Operating system:

    Windows physical or virtual server with the operating system 2003, 2008, and 2012

    Linux physical or virtual server

- **System suggested configuration:**
    - 4 GB of available RAM with minimum 500 MB of disk space
- **Role requirements**
    - MID Server user role
    - System administration of the server to install the actual MID Server
- **License requirements**: None

Now that we have gone through prerequisites for MID Server, let's now explore in detail step-by-step procedures to begin checking the prerequisites.

MID Server configuration and setup

Let's explore the steps required to configure MID Server connection prerequisites:

First step is to set up users and roles for MID Server. MID Server uses users and roles to interact with the ServiceNow instance through the SOAP web service. Best practice is to create individual user accounts for each of the MID Servers in the network that need to have a `mid_server` role to be able to access the restricted tables within ServiceNow.

Creating a MID Server role

Download the MID Server installation:

1. Log on to your server where you intend to install the MID Server.
2. Open the supported browser and log on to the ServiceNow instance, which is usually the developer instance.
3. Log on to the ServiceNow instance with your credentials.
4. On the remote Windows server navigate to **MID Server | Downloads**:

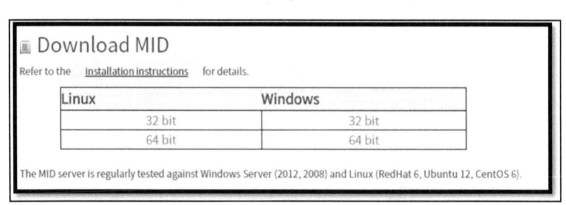

In this example, we will go ahead and download the 32 bit version. Now right-click on **Windows** and right-click on **32 bit** and then download to the server or the local machine where you are going to install the MID Server.

Creating an MID Server user

The next step is to create an user called `mid_server` to be able to work with the ServiceNow instance. The following are the steps to create a new user, `mid_server`, in the ServiceNow instance:

1. Log on to your ServiceNow instance.
2. From the left application navigator, navigate to **Users**:

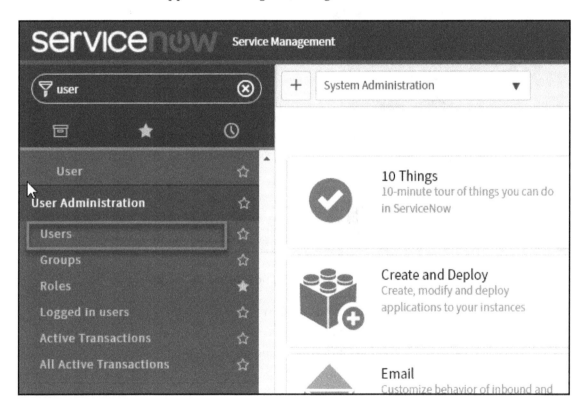

3. Now click on **New** to create a new user:

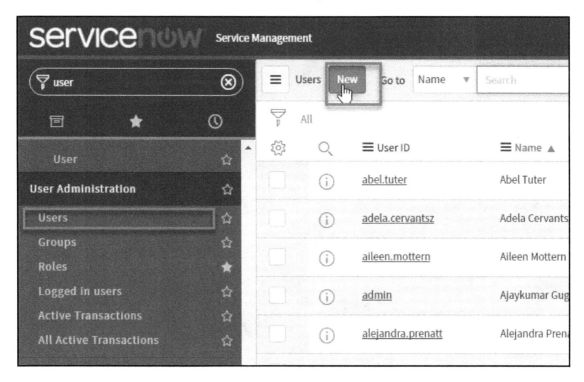

4. Fill in the required form files to create a new user:

- Provide the **User ID** as midserver
- Provide the **First name** as MID
- Provide the **Last name** as Server
- Provide the **Password** as midserver
- Please don't, you can provide any password that you wish to

- Right-click on the header bar and click on **Save**

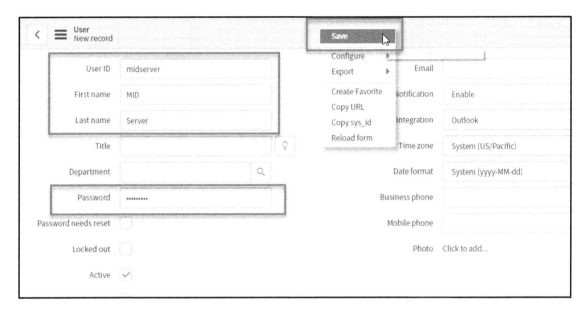

5. Scroll down to the bottom to the **Roles** tab , you will not see the **Roles** tab until you click on **Save**:

6. Now click on **Edit**.

7. Select the mid_server role for the left to the right selection box:

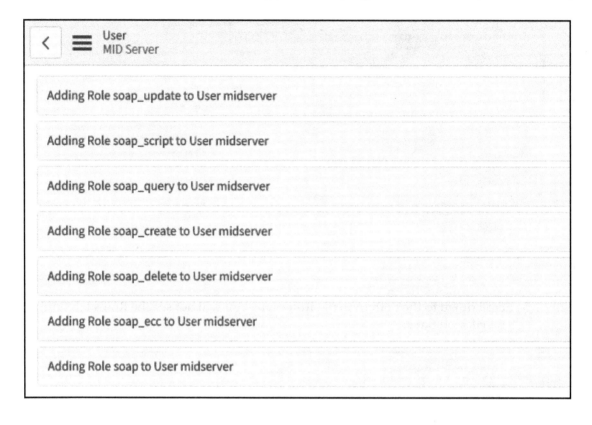

MID Server installation

Follow these steps to install the MID Server:

1. Create two folders in the root drive (example `C:` or `D:`)

2. Create a folder called `MID Server` in the root, the path to the folder will look like `C:MID Server`.

3. Now create one more folder called `MID Server 1` inside the newly created folder `MID Server`, the path to the newly created folder will look like `C:MID ServerMID Server1`:

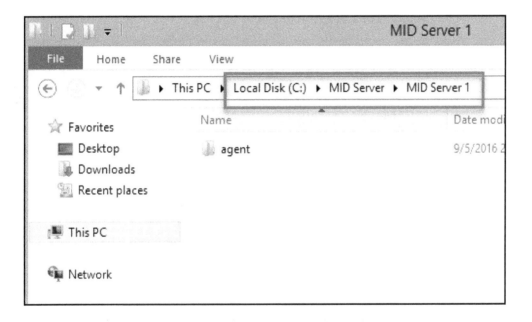

4. Extract the downloaded installation to the folder: `C:MID ServerMID Server1`

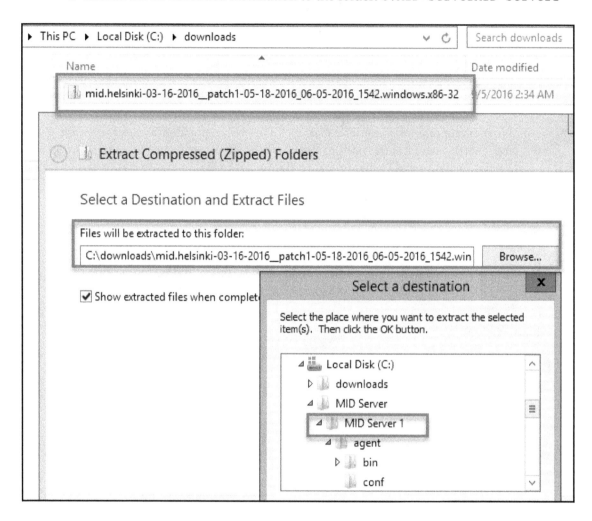

5. After extraction you will see a folder called `agent`:

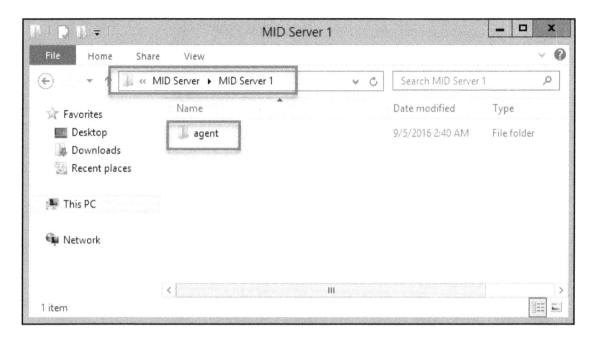

 The steps we have seen so far are common for a manual and automated installation. Now let's see the required steps for manual installation and we will later explain automated installation.

MID Server manual installation procedures

1. Open the folder called `agent` and you will see many folders and files inside the folder. Now right-click on the file called `config.xml` and click on **Open with | WordPad** or you can use any text editor:

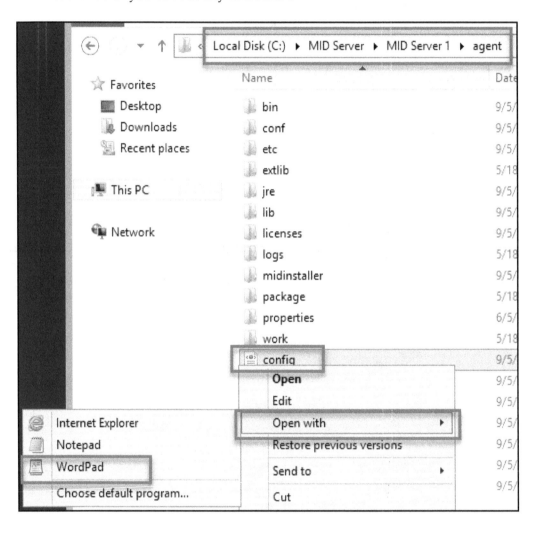

2. In the `config.xml` file you will need to provide the instance URL, login credentials, and MID Server name. Follow these steps to configure the XML file:

    1. To configure the instance URL, in the `config.xml` file scroll down to the XML tag section `<parameters>` and set the `parameter name =url` value as your instance URL example:

```
<parameter name =url value=https://dev24176.service-
now.com / |
```

    2. Now set the MID Server credentials as follows:

```
<parameter name=mid.instance.username value=midserver
/ |
    <parameter name=mid.instance.password value=midserver
    encrypt=true / |
```

    3. Now provide a name for the MID Server:

```
<parameter name =name value=MIDServer1 / |
```

```
        <!-- Tells the MID server where to contact its associated
Service-now instance.  Edit
        this value to provide the URL of your organization's
Service-now instance. -->
        <parameter name="url" value="https://dev24176.service-now.com"/>

        <!-- If your Service-now instance has authentication
enabled (the normal case), set
        these parameters to define the user name and password
the MID server will use
        to log into the instance.  -->

        <parameter name="mid.instance.username" value="midserver"
/>
        <parameter name="mid.instance.password" value="midserver"
encrypt="true"/>

        <!-- Defines the name by which your MID server is known on
the Service-now instance.
        Edit this value to provide the name you want, or
leave it blank and the MID server
        will make up a name. -->
        <parameter name="name" value="MID Server 1"/>
```

3. Now save the `config.xml` and close it.

Configuring the MID Server services

Follow the steps to configure the MID Server services:

1. Click on the start.bat file in the agent folder in MID Server 1, the path to the agent folder is C:MID Server MID Server 1agent.

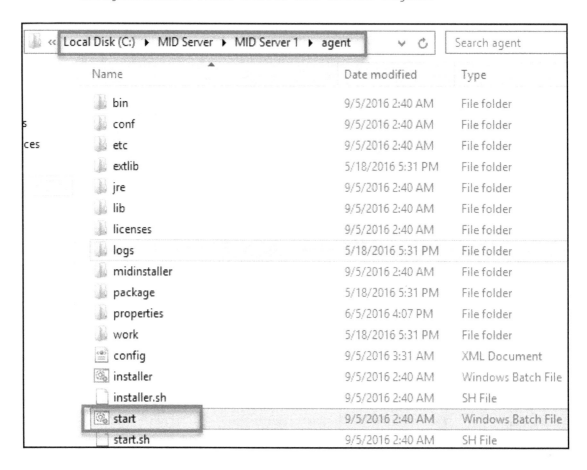

2. Right-click on the `start.bat` file and click **Run as administrator**:

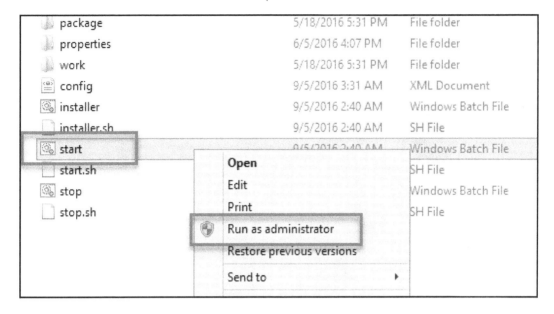

3. A command window will open and run the script:

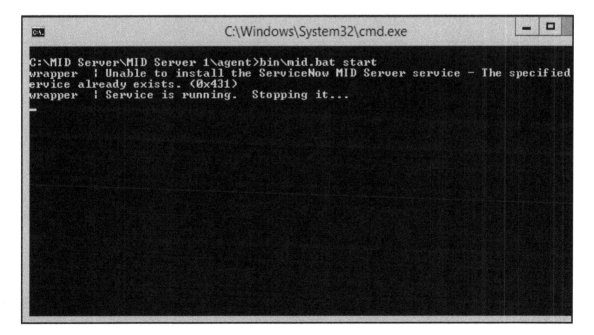

4. Navigate to **Administrative Tools** and locate and click on **Services**:

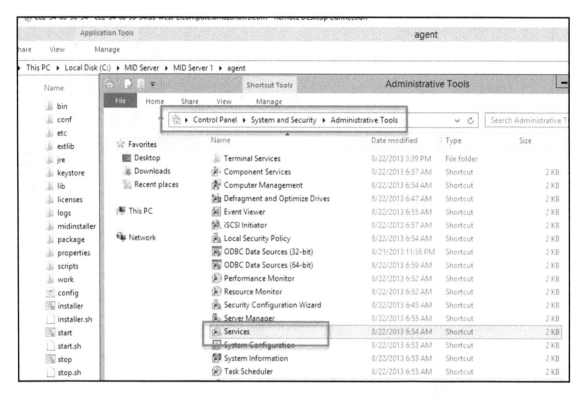

5. Locate the **ServiceNow MID Server** services:

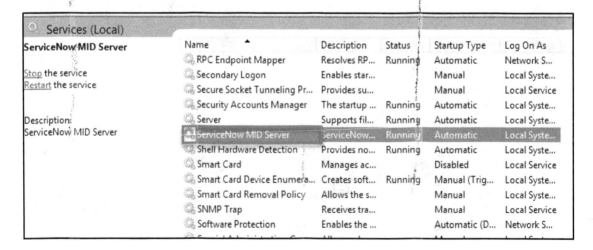

6. Right-click on **ServiceNow MID Server** and click on the **Log On** tab:

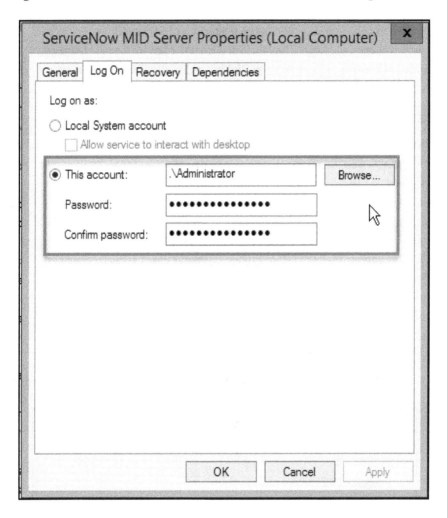

7. Now right-click on the **ServiceNow MID Server** services and click on **Restart**:

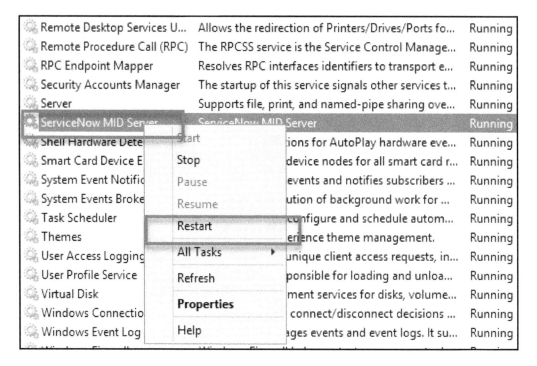

8. A progress bar appears when the **ServiceNow MID Server** gets restarted:

9. Now log back on to your ServiceNow instance:

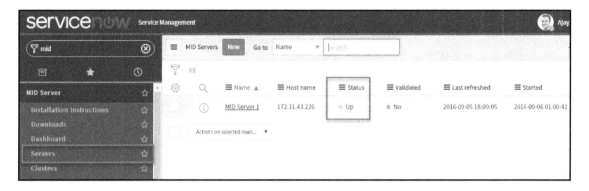

MID Server is now configured completely using manual steps. Now let's quickly see how to configure MID Server using automated steps.

MID Server automated installation steps

As we have seen the steps to install MID Server automatically, let's now see the steps to install MID Server in an automated way. Steps 1 through step 5 mentioned in *MID Server installation* are common for both automated and manual installation:

1. In the extracted folder, navigate to the `agent` folder and click on the `installer.bat` file:

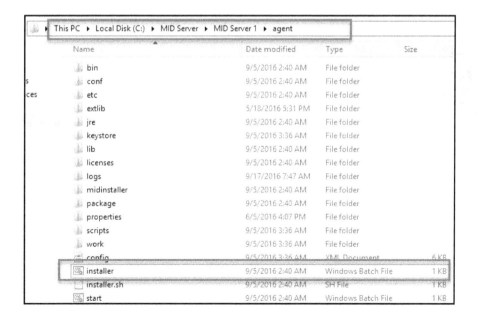

2. Right-click on `installer.bat` and click **Run as administrator**:

3. A command window will open up and an installation configuration screen will also open up:

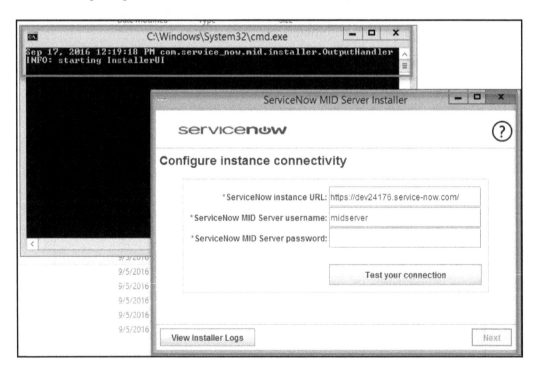

4. Fill in the required parameters in the form field:
   1. **ServiceNow instance URL**: URL to your instance.
   2. **ServiceNow MID Server username**: Username to the MID Server that you set on the instance.
   3. **ServiceNow MID Server password**: Password that you set to log on to the MID Server.
5. Click on **Start MID Server**. MID Server will be configured successfully. You will get a **Your MID Server has been configured successfully** message.
6. Clicking on **MID Server installer** will open the list of MID Servers, select the required MID Server.
7. Auto installation steps are completed and you will need to follow the following steps to validate the MID Server.

MID Server validation

Now that we have seen the steps to configure the MID Server, the next step is to validate the MID Server. By default, MID Server cannot execute any automation or orchestration tasks, MID Servers need to be validated, which enables restricting automation credentials to trusted MID Servers.

Once the MID Server is installed, you will notice that the Validated status is defaulted to **No**, in the following steps we will see how to change the MID Server to validated **Yes** state:

1. Open the installed MID server, for example, the **MID Server 1** that we had installed during the installation step:

2. Scroll down to the **Related Links** section and click **Validate**:

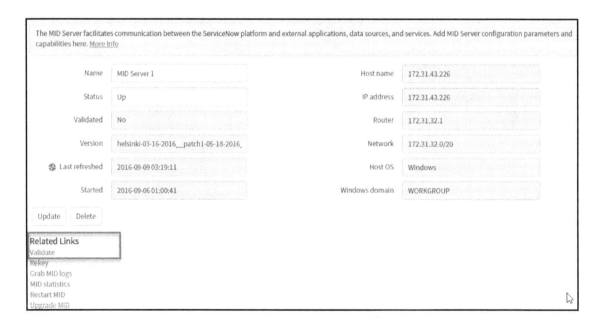

3. If you click on **Validation status** you will notice a prompt that says validation is in progress and the validation status turning green means the validation is completed:

MID Server is now validated.

Understanding related links

When you open the MID Server, you will notice various related links under the **Related Links** section, let's briefly see what these are:

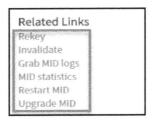

- **Rekey**: Forces the MID Server to generate a new asymmetric key pair
- **Invalidate**: Marks MID Server as invalid and forces asymmetric key generation
- **Grab MID logs**: Grabs the MID Server logs `wrapper.log` and `agent0.log.0`
- **MID statistics**: Opens all status of records in the ECC queue for this MID Server
- **Restart MID**: Restarts the selected MID Server
- **Upgrade MID**: Helps to upgrade the MID Server to the latest build stamp

Important MID Server connection parameters

MID Server settings can be adjusted to the way it should operate in the environment. There are different attributes that can be set for the MID Server. We will not be able to describe all the parameters in this book. When there is a specific need according to the environment you are setting the MID Server in, you might need to adjust the parameters accordingly.

How to set MID Server parameters?

1. Click on the **MID Server** from the application navigator:

2. By default, you will see the parameters that are already set for the MID Server. Be cautious in changing any parameters as that might impact the environment and the way MID Server works:

   1. In order to add a new parameter click **New**, which will open the attribute entry window.

   2. You can select the required MID Server you would like to set the attribute for in case of a multi MID Server environment. Clicking on the **Parameter name** will list all the available parameters that can be set for the MID Server; specific domains and values can be set for each of the parameters.

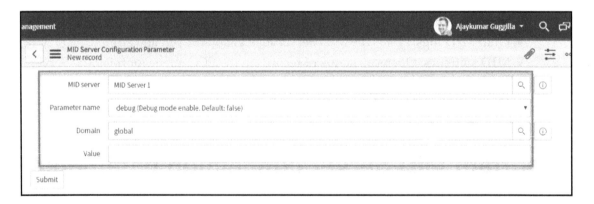

3. In the list of parameters, there are some that are restricted and cannot be changed, such as the following:

   - **mid.max.messages**: Maximum number of messages to hold in memory

- **instance.date.format**: Format that an instance uses for date and time
- **glide.mid.fast.responses**: Reduces time between a probe completion and response receiving
- **mid.jmx.enabled**: Enables management information to JMX consoles
- **glide.mid.max.sender.queue.size**: Maximum transmission queue size
- **threads.max**: Maximum number of probe threads
- **mid.poll.time**: MID Server pooling time

Setting IP ranges for MID Server

Imagine the IP range as your ZIP code and store selection. While searching for the closest store, we sometimes go to online maps or the store website to find the nearest store. We select the store we want to visit based on several factors including distance, product availability and so on. IP ranges for the MID Server work in a similar way; each MID Server will be given an IP range when there are multiple MID Servers in the environment. Different applications or plugins that leverage MID Server will leverage the right MID Server based on the given IP range, for example, there might be a MID Server for service mapping and there might be another MID Server for orchestration activities, specifying the IP ranges enables us to use the right MID Server in the environment:

1. To configure IP ranges, click on **IP Ranges** from the application navigator below the MID Server, and then click **New**:

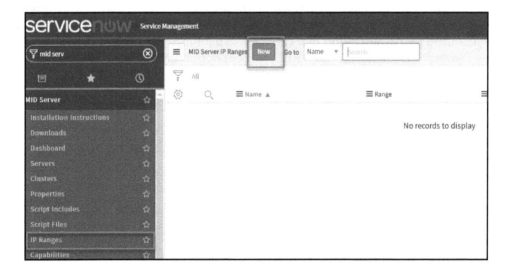

2. Clicking on **New** brings up a new window to enter specific values related to the IP ranges. In the **Type** parameter choosing **Exclude** will exclude the specified IP address range:

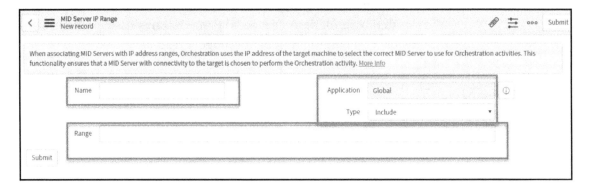

MID Server capabilities

There can be multiple MID Servers configured in a given range of IPs. Each of the MID Server can be leveraged for multiple purposes. For example, MID Server can be used for event management, MID Server can be used for orchestration, MID server can be used for discover and so on.

Imagine this as multiple vending machines in a store, some of them dispense movies, toys, drinks, keys, and so on. A vending machine is like an MID Server, each of the configured MID Servers can be used for a different purpose. Some ways to use a MID Server include MID Servers used for orchestration that can have capabilities not limited to SSH, SNMP, VMWare, PowerShell, and so on. Each MID Server should have at least one capability configured.

To configure the capability, follow these steps:

1. Open the MID Server from the application navigator and click **New** to add a new MID Server:

2. By default you will see some of the capabilities already in place. Clicking on **New** you can add a new capability:

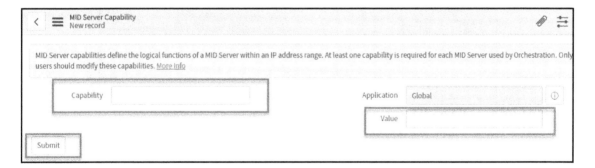

3. To add a capability to a MID Server, open the configured MID Server and scroll down to the section called **Capabilities**:

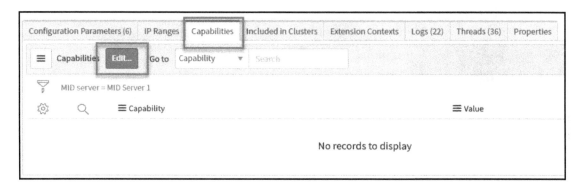

4. Clicking **Edit** brings up options for you to select the required capabilities for the MID Server:

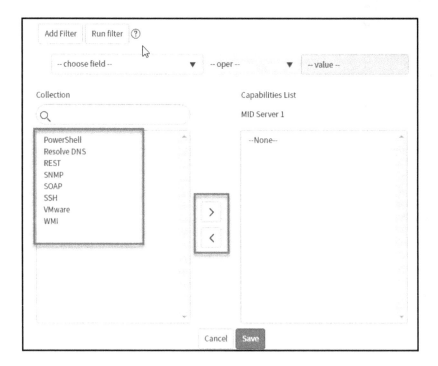

MID Server clustering

Unlike the high availability servers which mostly have the fail over or are for load balancing, even MID Servers can be configured for load balancing and fail-over protection. With this, we are able to cluster multiple MID Servers with the appropriate capabilities to be grouped together. Let's see how to set the clustering of MID Servers:

1. From the application navigator, click **Clusters** under the MID Server:

2. You can provide the **Name** and select the **Type** if it is going to be fail over or load balance:

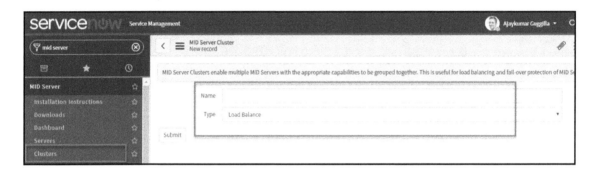

3. To add clustering options, scroll down to an existing MID Server, click on the **MID Server**, and navigate to the **Clusters** section and then click on **Edit**. Clicking **Edit** will bring up options to select a particular cluster:

With this we have completed configuring the MID Server and setting key attributes.

Summary

In this chapter, we have learnt about MID Server architecture, how to set up MID Server including a guided setup and the traditional way of manual configuration of MID Servers. Concluding, we also saw how to set some of the parameters for the MID server and MID Server capabilities.

3
Configuration Management Using ServiceNow Discovery

Configuration management is about managing the lifecycle of infrastructure components. **Configuration Management Database** (**CMDB**) has all the **Configuration Items** (**CI**) with its relationships. ServiceNow discovery plays an important role in populating the CMDB by discovering the configuration items for a given network. In this chapter, we will learn about ServiceNow discovery architecture, and how to configure and set up ServiceNow discovery.

What is ServiceNow discovery?

Discovery is a plugin within ServiceNow that helps in exploring a given network and identifies the interdependencies between the infrastructure components. Individual infrastructure component is refered to as configuration item or CI.

Discovery capabilities

Some of the discovery's capabilities include the following:

- It is able to discover and track assets and manage them
- It is able to find the application to infrastructure or application to application dependencies
- It is able to support the change management to do impact analysis by identifying the impact through the related configuration items

- It is able to identify new CI to populate the CMDB
- It supports the Service Mapping to map the business layer

The discovery application can find the following infrastructure elements in the network:

- AIX systems
- ESXi servers
- HPUX systems
- Linux systems
- Linux **Kernel-based Virtual Machines (KVM)**
- Apple MAC systems
- Netware
- Solaris systems
- Solaris zones
- Virtual machines
- Windows systems
- Apache web servers
- General software packages
- JBoss servers
- Microsoft IIS servers
- MySQL servers
- Oracle databases
- Tomcat servers
- Network printers
- VMware vCenter
- Websphere servers
- Network printers
- Network switches
- Network routers
- **Uninterruptible Power Supplies (UPS)**
- Load balancers
- F5 Big IP
- IP addresses
- IP networks
- Relationships
- Services and daemons

- Storage devices
- TCP connections

Discovery can classify and discover the following operating systems:

- AIX
- HPUX
- Linux
- Solaris
- Windows 2008 Server
- Windows 2008 Server R2
- Windows 2012 Server
- Windows 2012 Server R2
- Windows cluster VIP
- Windows 7
- Windows 8
- Windows 8.1
- Windows 10

Prerequisites

Following are some of the requirements for setting up the discovery application.

Required ServiceNow applications/plugins

Following are the two plugins required to set up the discovery application:

- **MID Server**: Create the MID Server user that has permission to connect to the ServiceNow instance
- **Credentials**: Create the credentials that the MID Server needs to communicate with devices in your network

Role requirements

An administrator with access to the discovery quick start application, access or be able to configure the MID Server, and also configure other key parameters including behaviors, probes, and sensors, and so on.

License requirement

Discovery is available as a separate subscription from the rest of the ServiceNow platform and it requires the discovery plugin.

In this chapter, we will follow the steps on how to set up discovery easily. To set up discovery easily, ServiceNow provides the discovery quick start feature to configure the required components within ServiceNow easily through wizards.

Configuring discovery the easy way

An easy way to start using discovery is to use *discovery quick start*, which is under the discovery application. It allows us to set up discovery easily to configure the MID Server, create credentials, and schedule discovery.

Activating the plugin

Follow the steps to activate the discovery plugin. The following steps describe how to activate a plugin on the personal instance. Separate steps need to be followed to activate the plugin for the commercial version of ServiceNow. Plugins are activated from the HI portal.

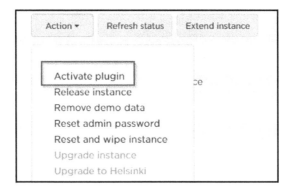

To activate the discovery plugin, the administrator has to do this from the instance management console:

These screenshots might vary from the actual instance for activating the plugin.

1. Click on **ACTIVATE**, which is next to **Discovery**:

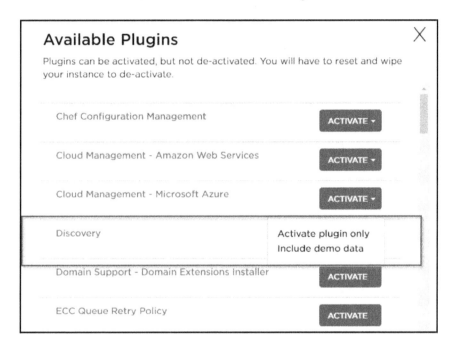

2. Once you activate the **Discovery** plugin, now you can navigate to the application navigator and type in **Discovery**. This will bring up **Discovery** applications and the options, as shown in the following screenshot:

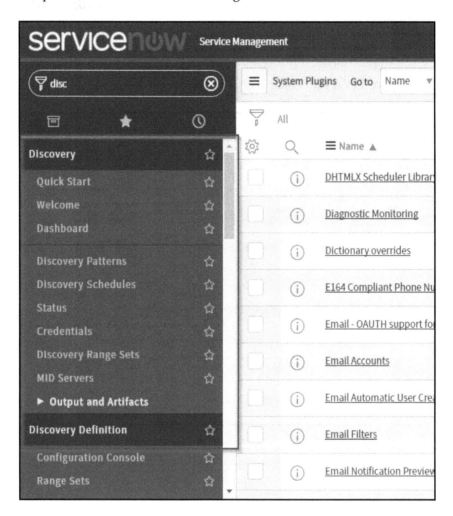

3. Under the **Discovery** application, click on**Quick Start**:

4. After you click **Quick Start**, the MID Server configuration console opens up:

5. In Chapter 1, *Introduction to IT Operations Management in ServiceNow*, you learnt and set up the MID Server, you can provide the same credentials to set up the MID Server if you are planning to leverage the same MID Server. If not, you can follow the instructions in Chapter 1, *Introduction to IT Operations Management in ServiceNow*, to set up a new MID Server.

If you have already installed the MID Server in Chapter 1, *Introduction to IT Operations Management in ServiceNow*, and chose not to install the MID Server and want to leverage the credentials in the **MID Server User** step once you have entered the credentials, you will need to wait for **2**, which is **Waiting for MID Server to connect....**

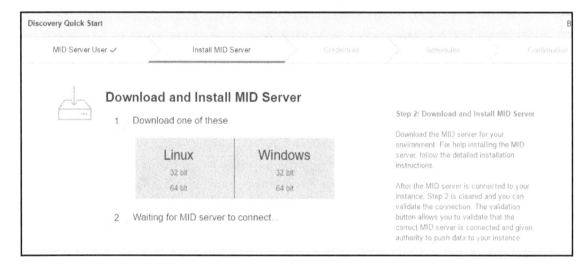

6. Once the MID Server is authenticated, you will receive a confirmation that MID Server is authenticated and connected to the MID Server for which the user credentials are provided:

7. The next step is to provide credential information that discovery will use to explore and scan the infrastructure components. Choosing the type will have different credential information:

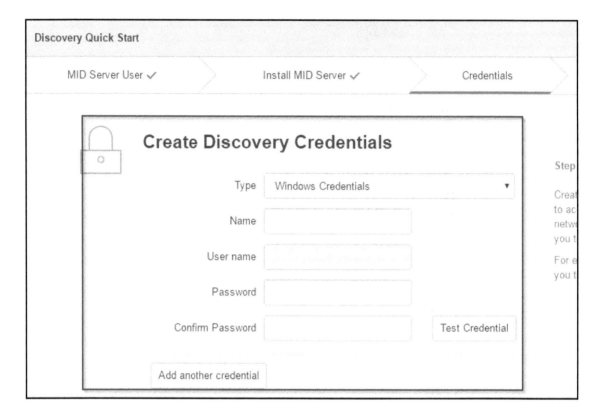

8. The next step is creating a **Discovery Schedule**; you will provide the information, such as when you want discovery to run and which IP ranges you would like to target discovery to run. In case of multiple MID Servers, you specify different IP ranges to discover the configuration items:

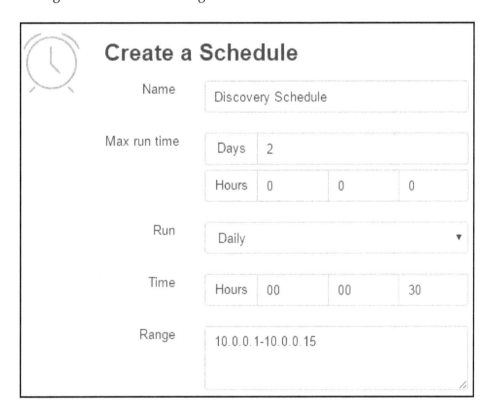

9. Once discovery is set up, you will receive a confirmation summary about the settings:

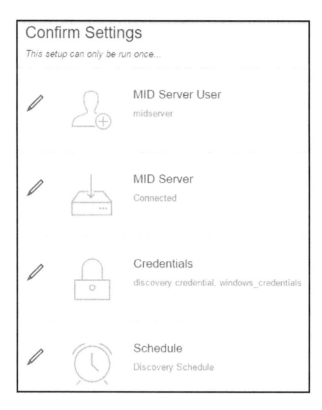

10. Once the discovery quick start setting has been completed, you will receive confirmation about completion and discovery is now ready to be scheduled:

Discovery credentials setup

Credentials are used by discovery, orchestration, and service mapping to access the external devices that they explore or manage. MID Server, which is installed on the Windows operating system, uses the login credentials of the MID Server service on the host machine to discover Windows devices. For Linux and Unix machines and network devices, the MID Server leverages the SSH and SNMP credentials.

Follow these steps to set up credentials:

1. Search for **discovery** in the application navigator, which will bring up all the existing credentials, or click **New** if you need to create a new credential:

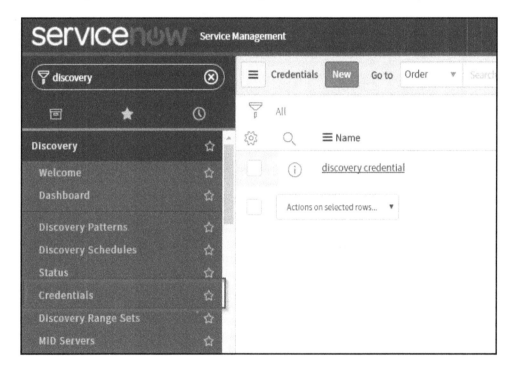

2. Next, you will have options to select what type of credentials we are trying to create:

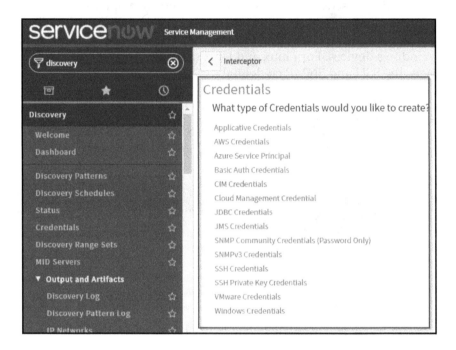

3. Click on **New**, which will open a new form to enter the values. Entering the required information and clicking on **Test credential** lets you test the credential:

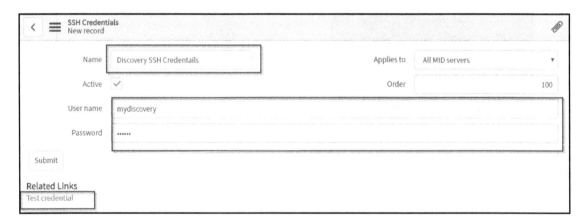

Discovery schedule

Discovery schedule will determine what the discovery run will search. Discovery schedule helps us with the following:

- IP address-based device identification
- Specifying if device probes will use credentials
- Configuring use of multiple MID Servers
- Manual discovery run
- Specifying an MID Server for a type of discovery

Follow these steps to configure the discovery schedule:

1. Search for **Discovery Schedules** on the application navigator that brings up all the existing schedules, click on the existing schedule to modify an existing schedule, or click on **New** to create a new schedule:

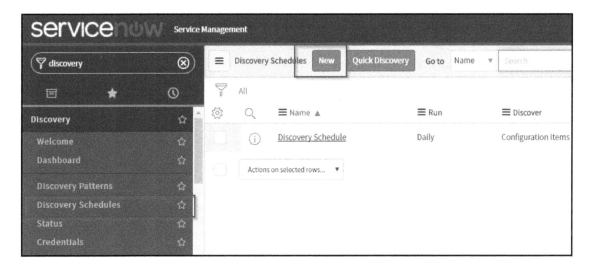

2. Click on **New** to create a new **Discovery Schedule**, you will be able to configure different parameters for these schedules. Some of the key values for configuring are:

- **Discover**: Discovers configuration items, IP addresses, networks, or web services.
- **MID server**: Specifies the MID Server to use for this discovery. This is used when there are multiple MID Servers available.
- **Include alive**: Includes an alive scan even when it is not active.

3. Click on **Quick Ranges** if you need to specify multiple IP ranges for the discovery. Clicking on **Quick Ranges** opens up a window to specify the IP ranges:

4. Click on **Discover now** to run the discovery schedule:

5. **Discovery Status** shows the status of the discovery run:

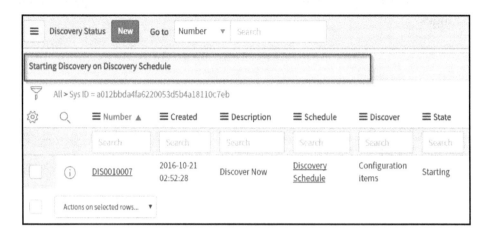

6. The **ECC Queue** tab shows the response back from the MID Server to the instance on the discovery:

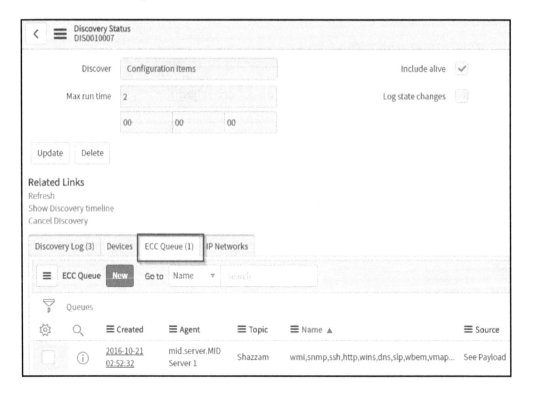

Discovery configuration console

The **discovery configuration console** lets you specify which devices and application types to ignore for the discovery.

Search for **Configuration Console** on the application navigator, which will open up a console to configure types to ignore or include for discovery.

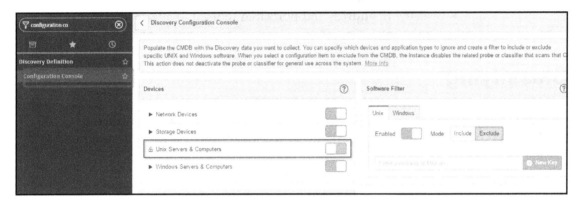

Discovery phases

The following are the different phases that are used to discover configuration items in the environment:

Scanning or port scanning phase

TCP and UDP IP ports are scanned by discovery to determine the open ports and also try to get responses from the ports that are open. WMI, SSH, and SNMP are the protocols that discovery searches responses from. Port scanning results are finally posted into the ECC queue.

Discovery follows through these steps of scanning the ports:

1. Find IP addresses with open ports with WMI, SSH, and SNMP protocol:
   - Lists the IP address in *Shazzam returns*
2. No response from the port:
   - Does not list the IP address in the returns in *Shazzam returns*
3. Refused connection from the port:
   - Lists the IP address and ports that refused in *Shazzam returns*

Classifying

Classify what type of device has been discovered that is available for IP address discovery type. Discovery classification occurs when a discovery is configured to discovery configuration items. This enables the discovery identifiers and it is the only scan used to update the CMDB.

When the discovery scanning is initiated at the first step and when the discovery has determined the device class, the discovery launches an identify probe or multi identify probe to run the command. The identity probe is the one that asks the device for attribute information on the device name, serial number, make, model, and so on.

Identification

After the device is classified and has found a match class, the scan results are processed by the identity sensor and passed to the identifier. The identifier tries to find a matching device in the CMDB and performs the following actions:

- **No match in the CMDB**: Creates a CI
- **Single match**: Updates the existing CI

- **Multiple match**: Stops

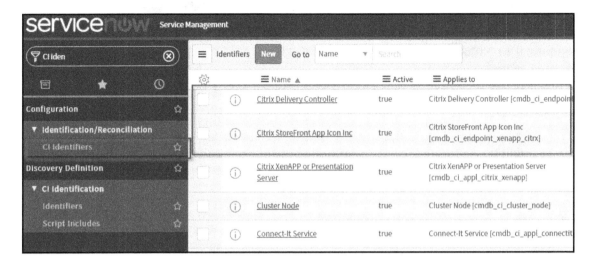

Probes and sensors

Discovery probes and sensors perform key tasks of data gathering and processing of the data that was gathered by discovery. Probe and sensor activities are controlled by the ECC queue. A job monitors the ECC queue, which looks for the ECC queue **output** and the **ready** state:

The output ECC messages are taken by the MID Server and processed, MID Server runs the necessary probes and returns the probe results to the ECC queue. The results from the probe are put back to the ECC queue as input entries. A business rule is fired on inserting data on to the ECC queue as input. The sensor processes the data that is required, which updates the CMDB.

Probes

Probes are responsible for collecting the information that is launched by the MID Server. A probe might be configured to get specific attribute information such as a configuration item name or a server IP address. An exploration probes return more specific information about the IP addresses.

Configuring probes

Probes can be configured from the ServiceNow instances, and attributes can be changed to what information is required and to be probed.

Steps to configure or modify probes:

1. On the application navigator, search for probes under the **Discovery Definition**. **Discovery definition | Probes**, on the content pane you will find the list of all the probes currently in place, click on any probe that you would like to modify, or click **New** to create a new probe:

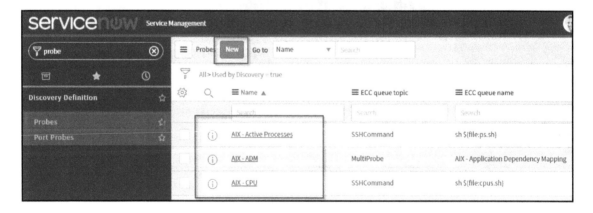

2. Click on any existing probe to modify, or click **New** to create a new probe. In this walk-through, we will open an existing probe. Setting different values on these probes might change the behavior of the probes, so you will need to understand more about what these fields are.

We will see some of the important fields available to configure a probe:

- **Class**: Type of probe to query on the operating system. Probe classes available are:
    - **CIM probe**: Used to query CIM Server using WBEM protocols
    - **Multiprobe**: Runs one or more simple or mix probes on different types
    - **SNMP**: Used for network devices
    - **WMIRunner probe**: Used for Windows devices

- **ECC queue topic**: Used for labeling ECC queue topics for incoming ECC queue messages. My default ServiceNow probe uses the following ECC queue topics:
    - CimProbe
    - Multiprobe
    - PowerShell probe
    - SCRelay
    - SSHCommand

- SNMP
- WMIRunner

- **ECC queue name**: The actual command the probe is to run.
- **Cache results**: Specifies to the cache probe the results in the probe results cache.

Port probe

The *Shazzam* probe uses the port probe to look for protocol activity on open ports on devices it comes across. When an open port is found, the *Shazzam* sensor checks the port probe to identify the classification probe to launch on that port, which might be SSH, WMI, SNMP, or something else. By default, the WMI probe is launched if the port does not respond to the WMI, then the SSH probe is launched to gather information about the device. Finally, when the port does not respond to the WMI or the SSH, the SNMO probe will allow identification if the device is running multiple protocols.

Now let's see how to configure the port probe scan:

1. Search for **Port Probes** in the application navigator, which will bring up ports that are already configured. Clicking on **New** lets you create a new port probe:

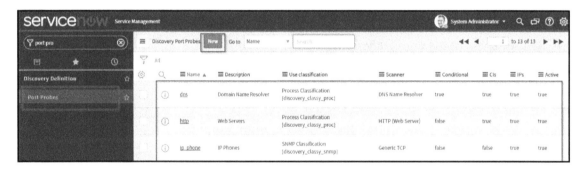

2. Click on any existing port probe to modify an existing configuration of a port probe. There are several options or settings to configure a port probe, changing options or settings will change the behavior of the port probe or it might not work as intended.

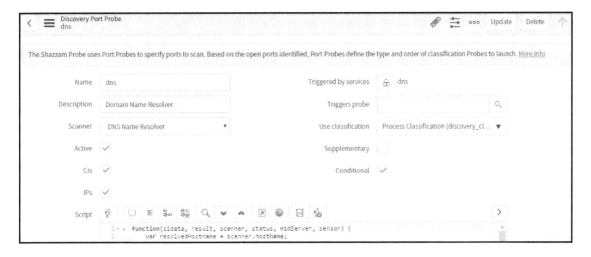

Some of the important configurations and settings are explained as follows:

- **Scanner**: The *Shazzam* scanner used to run on this port probe

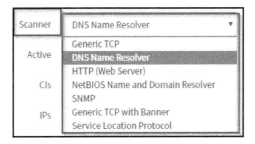

- **Conditional**: Enabled to resolve the names of the Windows device and DNS names when non-conditional probes return an open port
- **CIs**: Enabled or disabled for discovering configuration items
- **IPs**: Indicates whether this port probe is enabled or disabled for discovering configuration items

- **Trigger probe**: Name of the classify probe to use
- **Classification priority**: Specifies the priority in which the port probes must run

About sensors

Probes are used to identify and classify the device and gather information about the device, but there should be some mechanism to process the data, processing the data is taken care of by the sensors.

Let's take an example of mail coming in. In a post office, everyday they receive a bulk load of mail for a town, there are multiple post officers who will physically sit and process this mail based on area and street. Similarly, the data received by the port probes are like mail received, and sensors are the post officers that process the data of where to deliver and what to do.

Depending on the type of probe, the sensor is triggered accordingly.

Now let's see how to configure sensors and what the important attributes available are. Search for **Sensors** from the application navigator, clicking on **Sensors** opens up the list of sensors available. To configure a new sensor, click on the **New** button or click on any one of the existing sensors to modify attributes of an existing sensor:

1. Search for **Sensors** in the application navigator, clicking on the sensor brings up all existing sensors that are configured:

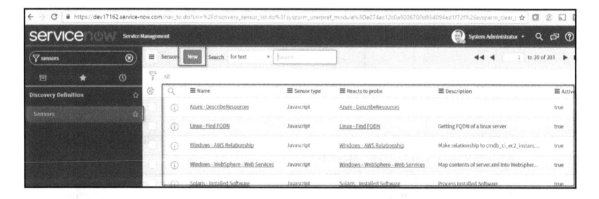

2. Click on any existing sensor to change any values or settings:

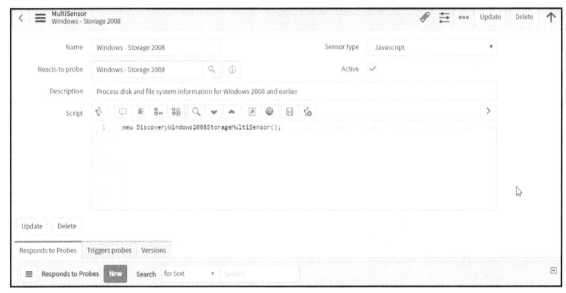

Let's see some of the important settings available to configure a sensor:

- **Sensor type**: Used to specify how the results should be processed the results that are returned from probe. Mostly JavaScript or XML is used. When using JavaScript, the data from the probe is processed within the sensor itself, which can be viewed. When selecting XML, the data from the probe is broken into pieces used to launch the other probes.

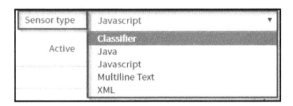

- **Script**: A script that needs to be run when processing a probe.
- **Sensor type**: Select the type of sensor to create. The most used ones are multisensor, multiprobe, and sensor.
- **Responds to probes**: Use this option to specify the probe to use within a multiprobe whose payload the multisensor must process.

- **Trigger probes**: Used to specify which probe the sensor uses for the exploration.

About ECC queue

The **External Communication Channel** (**ECC**) queue displays messages from and to the MID Servers, which are usually called **input** and **output** messages. The input messages are ones that are sent from the MID Server to the instance and the output messages are the ones from the instance to the MID Server:

1. To view the ECC queue, search for **ECC** in the application navigator, which will bring in all the messages in the ECC queue, the queue column specifies if the message is an input message or output message:

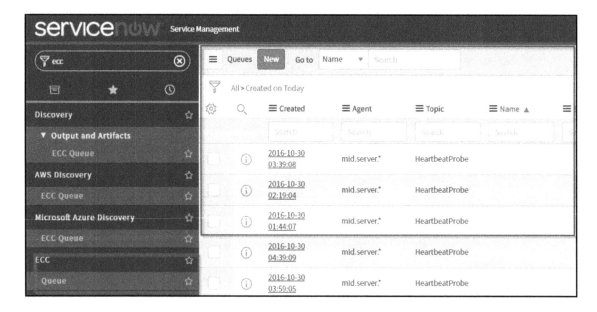

2. Clicking on any of the messages will open up details of the ECC message:

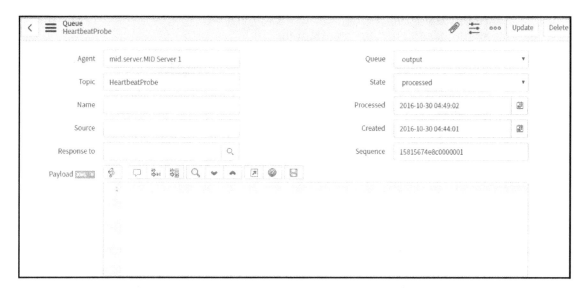

Let's see some of the key values or data that is received in the ECC queue:

- **Agent**: Name of the MID Server or system from which the message is received
- **Topic**: Name of the probe the MID Server is set to run
- **Source**: Contains the IP addresses that the probe is to run against
- **Payload**: Returns XML messages from the probes

Discovery pattern designer

To discover the devices and applications, the pattern designer creates a sequence of commands that are mostly preconfigured and can be customized. Each discovery pattern serves to discover only one CI type, but the discovery can use more than one pattern to discover the same CI type.

Let's see how to create an empty pattern and configure important settings:

1. Search for **Discovery Patterns** from the application navigator, which will bring up all the existing patterns configured:

2. Clicking on **New** opens up a form to create a new pattern. The settings or configurations available are:
   - **Name**: Name of the pattern
   - **CI type**: Select CI type for this pattern to discover, as mentioned earlier you can have one pattern for a CI type
   - **Pattern type**: Choose **Service Mapping** for service mapping patterns, select **Discovery Host** to discover a host, and select **Discovery Application** to discover an application running on a host

3. Click **Submit** to create the new pattern using basic options, advance attributes are available in the pattern designer window:

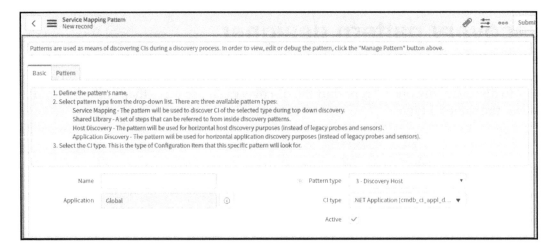

With this we have seen how to configure discovery and the different options that are available. There are a lot more settings than explained, we have just covered the core requirements to configure and set up discovery.

Summary

In this chapter we learnt about the important usage of discovery, learnt about the discovery architecture, explored the ECC queue, and saw how the discovery writes messages to the ECC queue. We also saw how to get started in setting up the discovery and finally we saw how to set important discovery attributes.

4
Creating and Managing Dependency Views

A dependency view graphically displays an infrastructure view for a configuration item and the business services that it is part of and that it supports. A dependency view indicates the status of its configuration items, and allows access to the CI related alerts, incidents, problems, changes, and business services.

 Starting from the Istanbul release, dependency maps are not separately called out in the ITOM suite of applications. Dependency maps are described separately in Helsinki and prior versions.

What are dependency views?

We have discussed dependency views with some examples in the first chapter. In this chapter, we will focus more on how to create and view dependency views. A dependency view shows a snapshot of how different logical and physical infrastructure items are connected and interrelated to one another. Logical grouping might be a business service, a reference to a process, or any other logical item whereas a physical infrastructure item might be any infrastructure component like a server, network device or any other infrastructure device.

Dependency views are like organization charts, which have upstream and downstream relationships such as a person whom he reports to or his supervisor and then the downstream relationship are like the person's reportee.

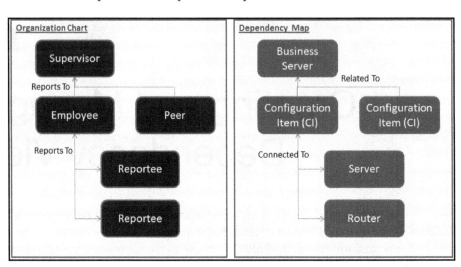

Now look at the following dependency map, which seems to be the same as the organization chart that shows upstream and downstream relationships of the configuration items:

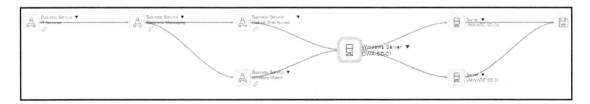

Dependency views have one root configuration item or CI; by default the dependency view shows the upstream and downstream CI. Administrators can configure the number of levels to be displayed in the dependency maps. In the dependency view maps there are map indicators, the map indicators indicate any active or any pending issues against a given CI, such as any active incidents, problems, or changes associated with a CI.

Many of the dependency relationships are automatically created by the discovery process; the created dependency views can be altered or deleted or a new dependency can be manually created.

Prerequisites for dependency views

Following are the basic prerequisites required to set up the dependency views

- **ServiceNow application**: The **Configuration Management Database (CMBD)** application must be enabled
- **Role requirements**:
    - Administrator or ITIL Role or custom role is able to access the CMDB tables. Administrator has the ability to create or modify dependency views map indicators, create or modify map icons, create or modify map related items, create or modify dependency views menu actions, and create or edit a dependency type.
    - Dependency views role required to access dependency view maps from the navigation menu, a script API, or directly from a URL.
    - The `ecmdb_admin` role is required to perform activities related to icons, indicator, and menu actions.

- **Browser requirements**:
    - The latest version or service pack of Internet browsers are required to view and manipulate dependency views maps

The dependency views module supports the latest version or service pack of the following browsers:

- Firefox with the latest ESR
- Chrome version 25 or later (latest version recommended)
- Safari version 6 or later
- Microsoft **Internet Explorer** (**IE**), with these requirements and limitations:
    - Dependency views requires IE version 9 or later
    - You cannot export images from a dependency views map using IE as your browser
- When you save a map view, dependency views will not make a thumbnail image. You may navigate to the saved map view using the version number.

Tables in dependency views

Dependency views add the following tables:

- `ngbsm_ci_icons`: Stores all available CI class icons.
- `ngbsm_ci_type_icon`: Maps icons to CI class names.
- `ngbsm_script`: Custom scripts that run in real time and generate a custom view of a map for a specific CI.
- `ngbsm_view`: Serialized map views saved by users.
- `ngbsm_filter`: Filters saved by users.
- `ngbsm_context_menu`: Default and custom context menu actions that appear when users right-click a map.
- `ngbsm_related_item`: Stores which reference fields should be treated as relationships when building the map. This allows users to include CI's that are related via a reference field instead of a relationship.
- `bsm_edge_color`: Color definitions to use when drawing the relationships between nodes based on relationship type.
- `bsm_indicator`: Stores all map indicators.
- `bsm_graph`: Details of maps.
- `bsm_action`: Actions on the map.

Properties in dependency views

Dependency views adds the following properties:

- `glide.bsm.max_nodes`: Maximum number of CI's to display on a map at once
- `glide.bsm.too_many_children`: Maximum number of child nodes to display
- `glide.ngbsm.filters_remove_filtered_items`: Filtered out items should be removed from the graph along with any disjoint children
- `glide.ngbsm.filters_run_layout_automatically`: When filters are changed, the graph will recalculate the layout using the currently selected layout algorithm
- `glide.ngbsm.filters_fit_to_screen_automatically`: When filters are changed, the graph should be fit to screen
- `glide.ngbsm.performance_allow_curves`: Allow links between nodes to be drawn using smooth curves (may impact performance)

- `glide.ngbsm.notification_display_time`: Amount of time in milliseconds that a notification stays on the screen in dependency views
- `glide.ngbsm.search_ci_limit`: Maximum amount of results displayed when searching for CIs in dependency views
- `glide.ngbsm.search_service_limit`: Maximum amount of results displayed when searching for services
- `glide.ngbsm.search_rel_type_limit`: Maximum amount of results displayed when searching for relationship types
- `glide.bsm.color.affect_neighbors`: Color of an affected neighbor node's label
- `glide.bsm.refresh_interval`: This property has no effect on the map, and remains for backward compatibility purposes only
- `glide.ngbsm.show_class_labels`: When available, the map should display the class labels for each CI

Dependency views map indicators

Map indicators are icons that are used to display details about a configuration item such as any associated events, outages, incidents, problems, or changes. By default the dependency view maps have indicators for the following:

- Incidents that are opened and active on that CI
- Alerts that are opened related to that CI
- Planned and unplanned outages related to that CI
- Problem records that are associated to that CI
- Change records associated to that CI

The level of information on the dependency view maps and configuring the dependency view maps can be controlled by the administrator through the settings menu.

Creating a new map indicator

Following are the steps on how to create a new map indicator:

1. On the application navigator, click on **Map Indicators** under **Dependency Views**.

2. A list of indicators will display, click on any of the indicators to open up and modify the indicator. To create a new map indicator click on **New**.

3. Important fields mentioned in the **Map Indicator** form are discussed in detail in the following list:

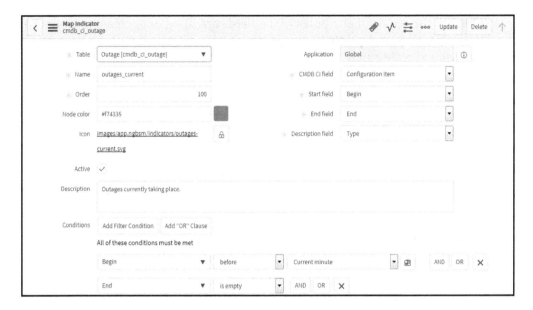

- **Order**: Priority order of the task.
- **Icon**: Filename and path of the icon image file, which can be a system image.
- **CMDB CI field**: Name of the field on the selected table that contains the configuration item.
- **Description field**: Name of the field on the selected table that contains the description of the configuration item.
- **Description**: Text to display when hovering over the indicator. Alphanumeric characters and spaces are valid for this field.
- **Conditions**: Condition builder that specifies for which CIs to apply this indicator. For example, a CI that has a current past outage is highlighted for five days. You can configure a condition to designate a different timeframe for what is considered to be current.
- **Active**: Checkbox to enable display of the indicator in a dependency views map.
- **Label**: Text to display for the indicator on the map.
- **Tooltip**: Label the prefix portion of the tooltip (**Tooltip Label**: **Tooltip info**).
- **Tooltip Info**: The suffix portion of the tooltip (**Tooltip Label**: **Tooltip info**).

4. Once all the required attributes of the fields are filled in to create or update a map indicator, click on **Update** to modify the map indicator or click on **Save** or **Submit** to create a new map indicator.

How to view dependency views

Following are the steps described on how to view the dependency views:

1. Dependency views can be viewed from the CMDB, opening up any CI record will show the dependency maps.
2. Search for any configuration item type from the application navigator, for example, search for Windows Servers CI.
3. Type in **windows** on the application navigator and click on **Windows**, from the list of **Windows Servers**.

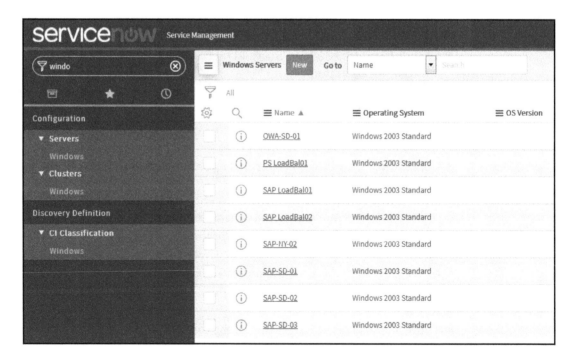

4. Click on any **Windows Server** name to open up the CI record and scroll down to the related items section.

5. Click on the dependency view icon to open up the dependency map, as shown in the following screenshot:

6. A dependency map will open up for the related configuration item or the CI.

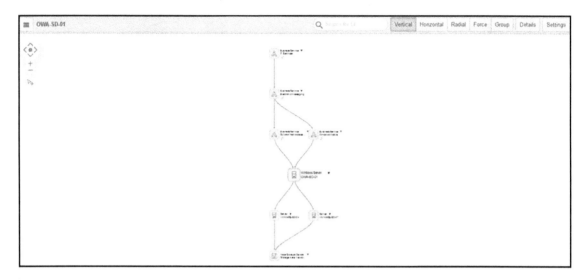

7. Dependency views maps contain the following menus and controls:

- Menu to save, load, and export views, as shown in the following screenshot:

- **Root CI**: Root CI appears next to the menu icon:

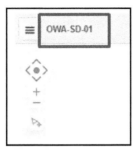

- Using the **Search for CI** feature you can load any configuration item or a business service into the dependency map view:

8. Dependency maps can be viewed by different positions by using the buttons that are available on the dependency maps, as shown in the following screenshot:

The following is a description of each of the options available:

- **Vertical**: Click to display the map in a vertical position:
- **Horizontal**: Click to display the map in a horizontal position:
- **Radial**: Click to display the map in a radial view:
- **Force**: Click to display centers the elements on the parent CI
- **Group**: Groups the elements according to their CI type
- **Details**: To display related lists such as problems, changes, and related business services:

9. When you click on the **Setting** icon, there are different options available:

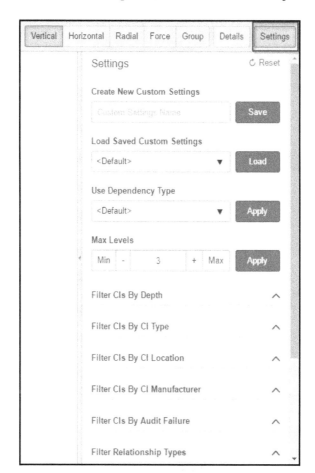

10. Dependency maps can be magnified using the following icons:

- Use the plus sign (+) to magnify the map
- Use the minus sign (-) to decrease the magnification
- To center the map, click the center of the map
- Use the direction arrows to move the page in the direction of the arrows

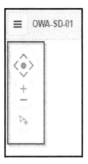

11. Right-click any icon on the dependency map to see other options available related to the selected CI:

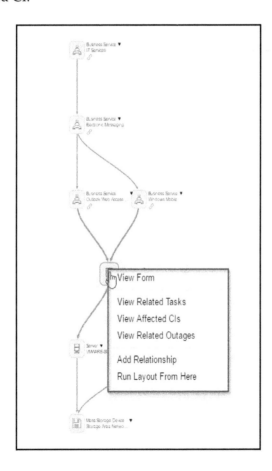

12. The following are the different options that you will see when you click the node menu:

    - **View Form**: Click it to display the CMDB record of the selected CI:

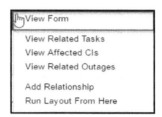

Clicking on **View Form** opens up the CI information where you are able to set different attributes for the selected configuration item:

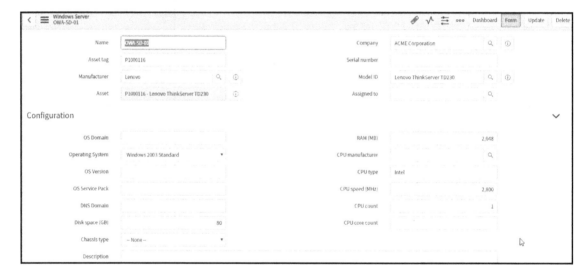

    - **View Map**: Click it to reload the map.
    - **View Related Tasks**: Click it to display the associated incidents, problems, changes, tasks, or any outages associated with the configuration item or CI:

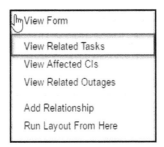

By clicking on **View Related Tasks** you can view all the tasks associated with the particular configuration item.

Clicking on the task number will open up the task information:

- **View Affected CIs**: Click on this to view all the tasks that have the CI as the affected CI:

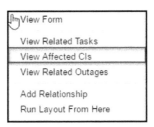

Click on **View Affected CIs** to see all the CIs that are affected.

By clicking on **Add** you are able to relate a CI as an affected CI:

- **View Related Outages**: View all outages associated with that particular CI:

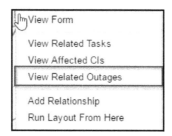

By clicking on **View Related Outages**, you will be able to view all the outages associated with the particular configuration item:

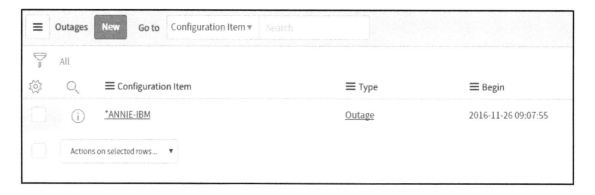

Clicking on **New** will bring up a window where a new outage can be entered:

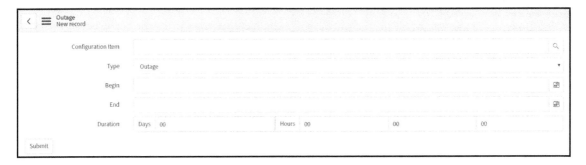

- **Run Layout From Here**: Rerun the layout using the current node:

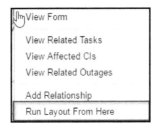

13. Creating relationships:
    1. To create a relationship, right-click on any CI and then click **Add Relationship**:

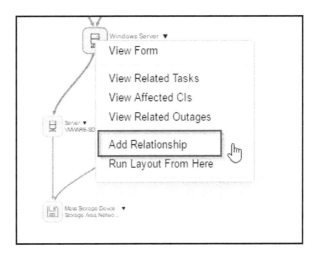

2. Once you click on **Add Relationship** you will see a green dotted line floating from the selected CI.

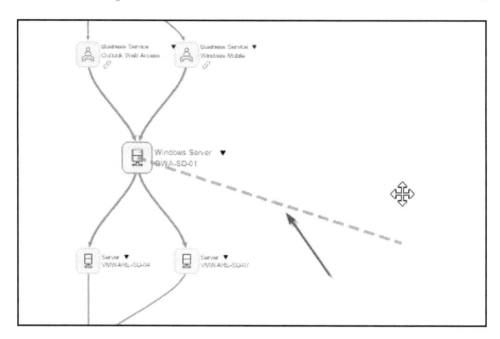

3. Now drag the floated line to a CI on the map to which you want to create a relationship to. Once you click on the destination CI you will see a window to specify the type of relationship, where you will be able to search for the type of relationship required for the particular CI:

How to save or load dependency map views

Following are the steps on how to save or load dependency map views:

1. Navigate to **Dependency Views** | **View Map**:

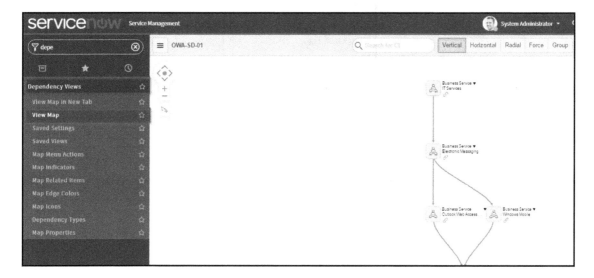

2. Click on the menu icon:

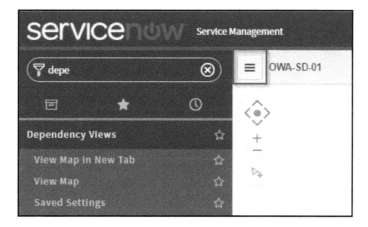

3. When clicking on the menu icon you will find different options to save and load the dependency maps:

4. A particular view can be saved using **Save View**, once you click **Save View** the screen will be saved:

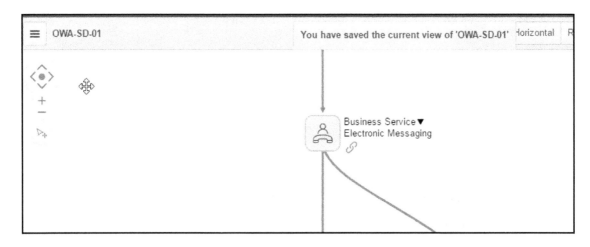

5. Clicking on **Load View** will give you a different saved view that you can choose to load. Clicking on any view will load the view:

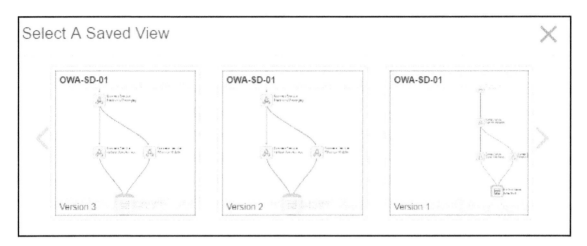

6. By clicking on **Export Image** you will be able to export the image and save it to a local folder.

7. The saved views can be accessed from the application navigator too. Navigate to **Dependency Views | Saved Views**:

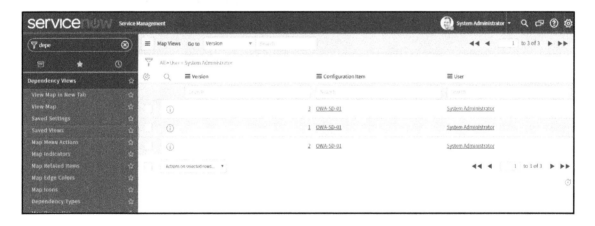

8. A list of all the saved views will be displayed here. You will be able to click on any view and delete any view:

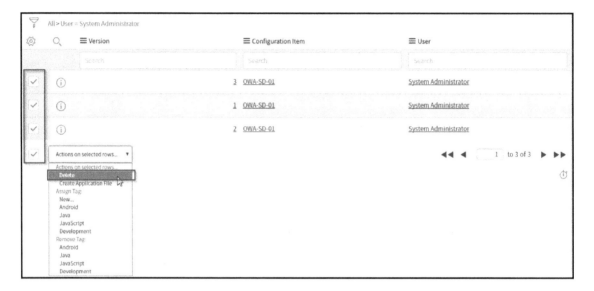

How to filter a view of a dependency view map

Following are the steps on how to filter a view of a dependency view map:

1. Navigate to **Dependency Views** | **View Map** on the application navigator:

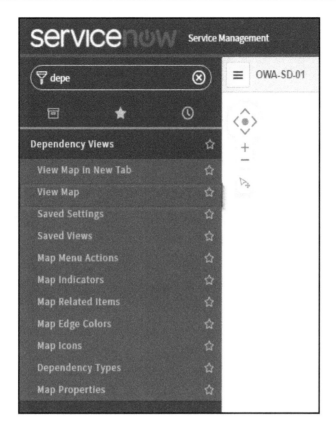

2. Now click on **Settings**:

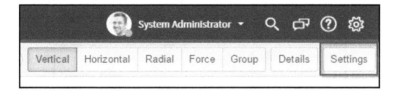

3. By clicking on **Settings**, you will find different options:

4. You can use these settings appropriately as required, some of the important settings are as follows:
   - **Create New Custom Settings**: Use this setting to create custom settings:

   - **Load Saved Custom Settings**: Use this option to load any saved custom settings:

5. Clicking on **Filter CIs by Depth** designates which levels of CI to display on the map:

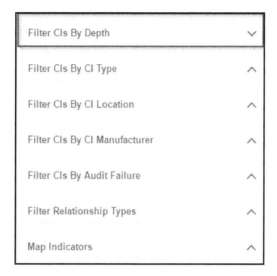

6. Following are the options available for the dependency maps:
    1. Clicking on **Filter CIs by Type** specifies what CI types to display.
    2. Using the tab filter you will be able to filter a specific configuration item.
    3. Use **Filter CIs by CI Location** to specify which CI locations to display on the map.
    4. Use **Filter CIs by CI Manufacturer** to specify what manufacturer to display on the map.
    5. Use **Filter Relationship Types** to specify what relationship types to display on the map.
    6. Use **Map Indicators** to specify what type of tasks to display on the map, for example, incidents, problems, changes, and so on.

Summary

In this chapter, we have covered how to view dependency maps and also how to customize dependency maps, detailed dependency indicators, and so on.

5
Cloud Management

In this chapter, we will learn about the cloud management application with ServiceNow. The cloud management application has made it very easy to manage virtual cloud resources easily, including making them available on the service catalog for people to subscribe to for the virtual resources. The cloud application has provided easy options to easily integrate with major cloud providers including Amazon AWS, Azure, and VMWare clouds. In this chapter, we will learn about:

- **Overview and understanding cloud management applications**: In this chapter, we will learn about the cloud management application and some important features in the application
- **Integrating with different cloud providers**: In our chapter, we will explore and integrate with Amazon AWS cloud and also touch on how to configure the other cloud providers
- **Integrating service catalog for cloud provisioning**: We will see how to create a service catalog using approved images.

Understanding cloud management applications

Managing the cloud instances had been difficult in the past, but nowadays it is easy to manage the cloud instances easily ServiceNow cloud management application. The ServiceNow cloud management application can be easily integrated with the major public cloud providers and also enables you to manage private clouds.

In this chapter, we will be exploring and walking thorough the steps on how to configure the Amazon AWS cloud application. The **Amazon Web Services** (**AWS**) cloud application allows you to manage the AWS products and services including:

- Amazon VMs
- Amazon **Elastic Block Stores** (**EBS**)
- Amazon **Virtual Private Clouds** (**VPCs**)
- Amazon CloudFormation
- Amazon tagging
- Amazon billing

There are different resources available on the AWS cloud application. The following picture shows the mapping between Amazon resources and the different applications within ServiceNow and how they are consumed.

- **Billing**: The data is consumed by the reporting to generate cost and usage reports
- **Cloud Watch** and **AWS Config**: The data is federated into the CMDB for the Service Watch use
- **EC2**: This is available for the ServiceNow orchestration use, which is finally integrated with the service catalogs

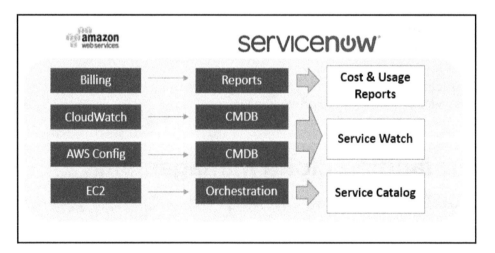

There are different steps for setting up your cloud application. Here is a sequence of steps to complete to set up your cloud application:

- Activate the Amazon web services plugin
- Create users and roles
- Registering the cloud
- Discover
- Create the catalog
- Provisions

Exploring integration with different cloud providers

We can activate the Amazon web services plugin as follows. Following are the steps to activate the Amazon cloud plugin, and the following screenshot is from the developer instance. Follow the steps to activate the required Amazon plugin:

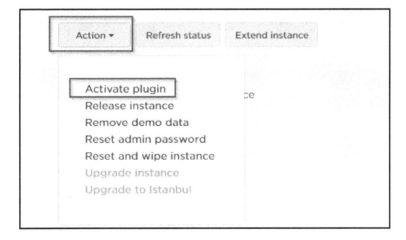

1. Search for the **Cloud Management - Amazon Web Services** plugin and click on **Activate.**

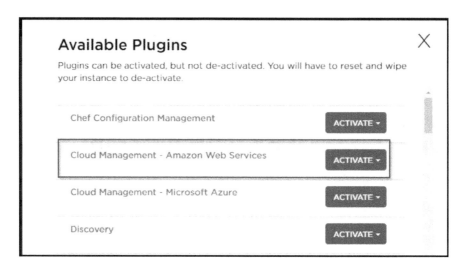

2. This is a personal developer instance, so click on **Activate plugin only** to activate the plugin.

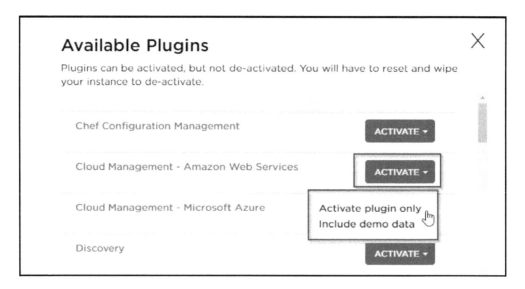

3. Installing the AWS plugin will install the following:
   - `com.snc.aws`: The primary Amazon AWS Cloud plugin
   - `com.snc.aws.activities`: Amazon AWS Cloud activities
   - `com.snc.aws.common`: Amazon common
   - `com.snc.aws.core`: Components common to Amazon AWS Cloud

 If you need to install Microsoft Azure and VMWare related-cloud applications, use the same to search for the following plug in and activate them.

4. To configure the Microsoft Azure application you will need to activate the following plugin:
   - Cloud management - Microsoft Azure
   - Microsoft Azure management application

5. To configure the VMWare virtual resources you will need to configure the following plugin:
   - Orchestration - VMware support
   - Orchestration activities - VMware

Users and roles creation

There are specific roles available for managing your cloud applications and specific resources. There are three different types of cloud users which are common for all the cloud providers or when managing virtual resources.

- **Cloud administrator**: Who sets up the system
- **Cloud operator**: Ensure provisioning and management
- **Cloud user**: Requests virtual resources

Role-based assignment needs to be done to provide the user with the right role. A user belongs to a user group and the cloud-related role is given to the user group. There are three different types of user groups:

- **Cloud user group**
  - **User group**: Virtual provisioning cloud users
  - **User role**: cloud_user

- **Privileges**: Requests virtual resources from the service catalog and uses the *my virtual assets portal* to manage virtual resources that are assigned to them
- **Cloud approver group**
    - **User group**: Azure Approves , EC2 Approves, VMware Approves
    - **User role**: ITIL
- **Cloud operator user group**
    - **User group**: Virtual provisioning cloud operators
    - **User role**: cloud_operator
    - **User group**: EC2 operator
    - **User role**: ec2_operator
    - **User group**: Azure operator
    - **User role**: azure_operator
    - **User group**: VMware operator
    - **User role**: vmware_operator

- **Cloud administrator**: Cloud administrators can monitor the cloud management environment using the cloud admin portal
    - **User group**: Virtual Provisioning cloud administrators
    - **User role**: cloud_admin, cloud_user, itil

Cloud operations portal

The **Cloud operations portal** is available to the cloud administrator and the cloud operator who have a view of all the cloud resources in a single view. To access the cloud operations portal, navigate to the following:

1. Type `cloud` in the application navigator.
2. Under **Cloud Management**, click on **Cloud Operations Portal.**
3. Clicking on the **Cloud Operations Portal** opens a dashboard on the content pane.

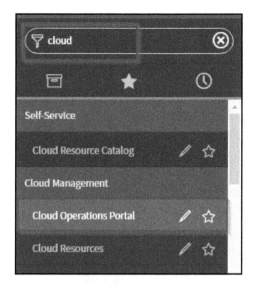

4. The cloud portal has a dashboard that has several different views available:
   - **Overview**: Gives a snapshot of all the virtual resources available, such as storage volumes, stacks, and release renewal information
   - **Resources**: Displays the virtual resource based on each cloud provider
   - **Requests**: Displays all the requests raised by the cloud users
   - **Missing tags**: Reports resource's missing tag value assignments

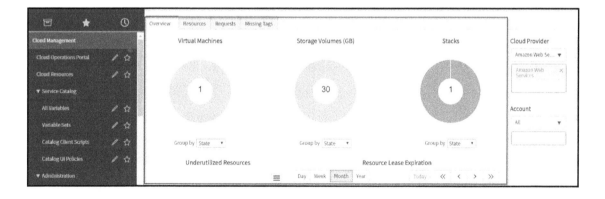

Configuring Amazon AWS cloud

AWS cloud administrators are able to configure the AWS cloud application. After the cloud administrator has started on this, the first step is to get the following information from the Amazon AWS account:

- Account IT
- Access key ID
- Secret access key

The following steps are from an Amazon AWS account:

1. Collect the AWS credentials account settings from the associated Amazon account.

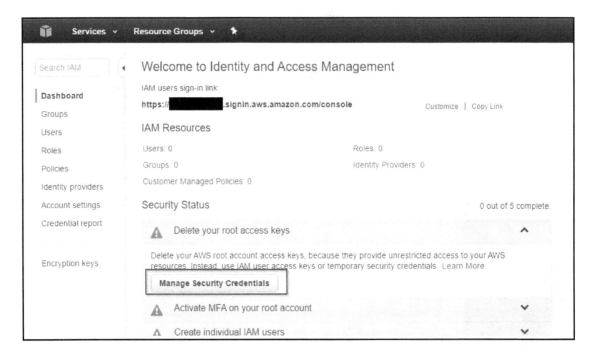

2. The next thing is to go to **Security Credentials** and click on the **Access Keys (Access Key ID and Secret Access Key)** to get the keys.

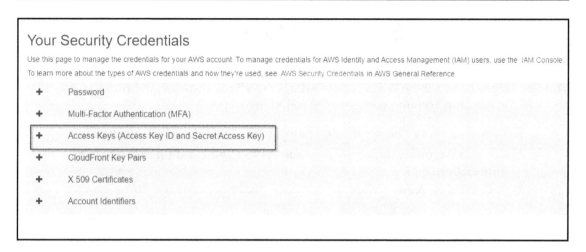

3. By clicking on **Create New Access Key**, you are able to create a new access key and a secret key.

Adding the AWS account to the ServiceNow instance

The next step is to add the AWS account to the ServiceNow instance. In order to configure and add the Amazon account, complete the following steps:

1. Type Amazon on the application navigator to open the AWS application.
2. Click on **Accounts** under the **Amazon AWS Cloud** and fill in the required information.
3. Now click on **New**.

4. Clicking on **New** opens up a form for entering the AWS account information. Enter a **Name** for the AWS account and the **Account ID**. You can get the AWS account ID from your Amazon AWS account. Click on the requested information and click on **Submit**.

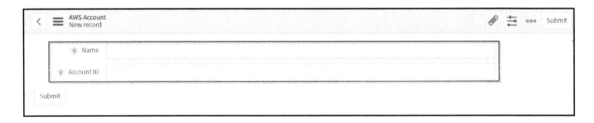

5. Right-clicking on the header and clicking the **Save** button gives additional options for you to enter the **Primary AWS Credential**. Clicking on the magnifying glass icon brings up additional options for selecting an existing AWS Account Credential or enabling you to enter a new credential.

6. On the **AWS Credentials** window, click on the **New** button to create an AWS credential.

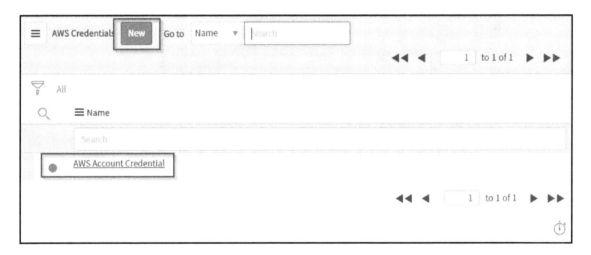

7. Options appear to enter information related to the AWS credentials, so enter the required information and click on **Update** button.
    - **Name**: Meaningful name for the AWS account
    - **Active**: Enable the AWS credential
    - **AWS Account**: You are able to select the AWS account against which the AWS credential is created
    - **Access Key ID**: Got from the Amazon AWS account
    - **Secret Access Key**: Got from the Amazon AWS account

8. Once you have filled in the required information, click on **Test Credential** to test the AWS credentials.

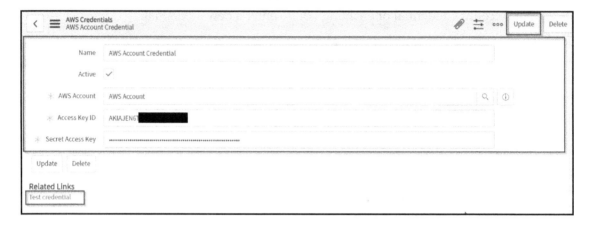

9. Once you click on **Test Credential**, you get a prompt about the validation's success.

How to create and customize an image permission

If the AWS account has images created and is able to access the images, we can configure the account to receive these images into the account.

In order to add shared image accounts to this, follow the steps:

1. Click on the related link **Shared Image Accounts** link; by clicking on this link you see a **New** button next to the option **Shared Image Accounts**.

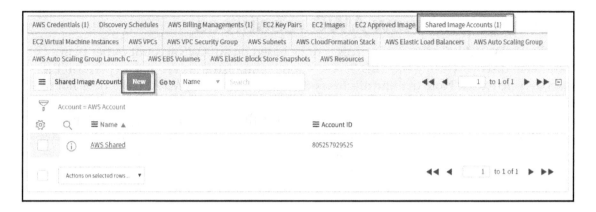

2. Clicking on **New** opens up a form. We need to fill in the following details in the form:

   - **Name**: Meaningful name for the shared image account
   - **Account ID**: AWS account ID
   - **Account**: The AWS credential for this shared image account
   - **Active:** Clicking on active we are able to make this shared image account active or inactive

3. Once you have all the information entered, click on the **Update** button to save the information.

Discover and view AWS resources

The discovery of AWS virtual resources is done based on an AWS account rather than traditional discovery using the MID Server. Cloud administrators are able to perform the discovery activities. Note that the discovery is done trough the AWS API and does not use the MID server at all.

A discovery schedule is capable of discovering more than one AWS account. With the help of MID Server, a host-based discovery of virtual hosts can also be performed. The MID server needs to be placed in the AWS cloud, but the host discovery may not be as rich as *normal* discovery due to limitations in the AWS cloud. You can follow `Chapter 2, MID Server Essentials`, to learn how to configure and set up a MID Server.

Let's now create a discovery schedule; to create a discovery schedule, perform the following steps:

1. Navigate to **Amazon AWS Cloud** I **AWS Discovery** I **Accounts**. Click on an existing account or click on **New** button to create a new one. Now click on **AWS Account**; it is the existing AWS account that we had created.

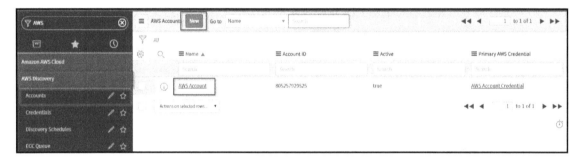

2. Clicking the existing **AWS Account** opens up the form. Now scroll down to the related list below and click on **Discovery Schedules**, or you can click on the related links **Create Discovery Schedule**. You can click on create **New**.

3. Clicking on **New,** you are able to create a new discovery schedule. There are certain fields that need to be filled in.

   - **Name**: Name of the discovery schedule
   - **Discover**: There option available in a **Web Service**
   - **MID Server**: You are able to select a MID Server if the discovery is going to be a IP based, if not the AWS account based discovery will be done.
   - **Active**: To make enable to disable the discovery schedule

- Schedule: **Max run time**, **Run**, and **Time** are some of the options available to provide a schedule

4. Once you enter the required information, you can click on **Discover now** to start discovering the AWS resources based on the given credentials.

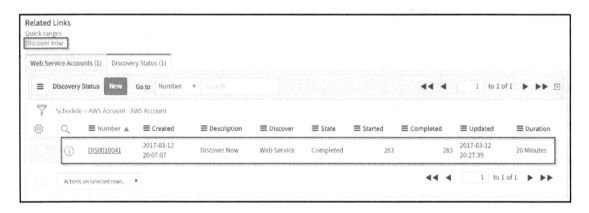

5. If there is no MID Server selected, the AWS discovery starts and you are able to see the status of the discovery.

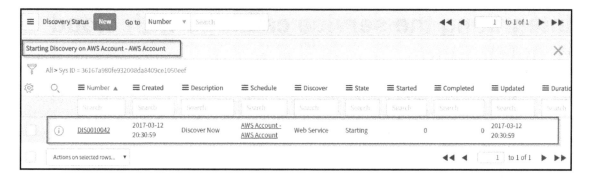

6. Once the AWS discovery runs, you can notice in the related list that there are numbers filled in after the AWS discovery has run. The related tabs are filled in based on what is available and subscribed to in the AWS account. You will get an error saying **com.glide.attachment.max_get_size** is too small. This property sets the maximum size of the payload, and in most cases the default size of this property is too small for getting all the details from the cloud provider. Default is 5 MB, and this needs to be extended to match the size of the current implementation.

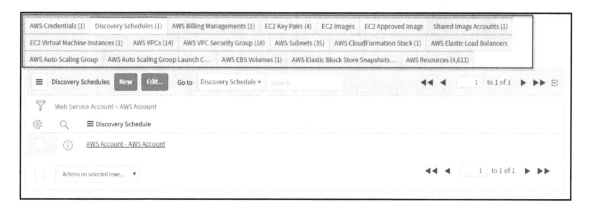

Integrating the service catalogs with cloud provisioning

In this chapter, we will see how to integrate the service catalog with cloud provisioning.

1. The first step is to create the sizes; to create the sizes, follow the steps to set up the service catalog for the AWS cloud offering.

2. Clicking on **New** opens up a form to fill in the EC2 size.

 These sizes are available on the Amazon AWS website, usually located on the AWS pricing chart.

3. Images need to be approved before they are available to create a service catalog. Follow the steps to approve the images that have been created:
    1. Type `aws` under the **Amazon AWS Cloud** application to search for **Available Images**. Click on **Available Images**.

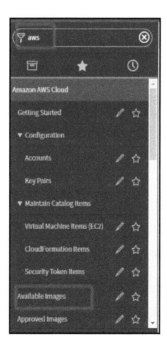

2. Clicking on **Available Images** will list all the available images. Click on any available image to open it.

3. Now click on the **Approve** button to approve a particular selected image. When approving an image this makes it possible to create a catalog item from it.

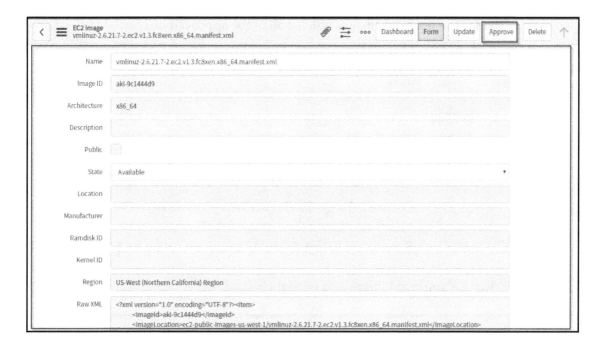

4. All approved images are available under **Approved Images**. Clicking on that lists all the approved images.

5. Clicking on **Approved Images** will list all of the approved images, so click on any image and open the record.

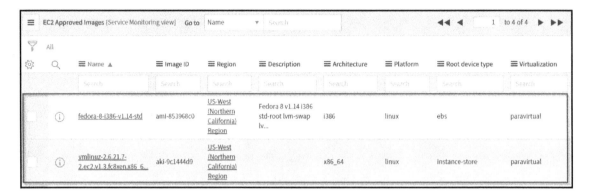

6. Click on an approved image and open the record.

7. Scroll down to the bottom under, and under **Related Links** click on **Create Catalog Item**. Fill in the required information and click on the **Update** button to save the information.

8. After you have enter all the information required, click on the **Publish** button to publish the service catalog.

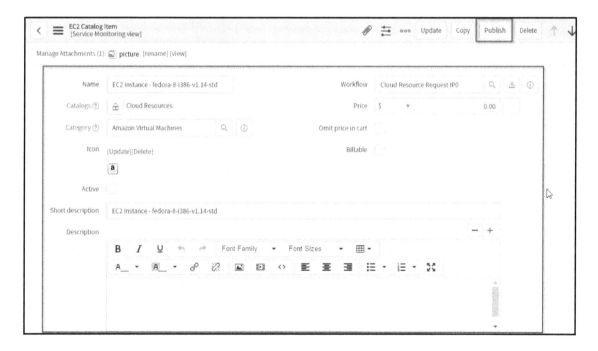

9. Once the service catalog is published, you can click on the following link to view all the AWS catalogs that have been published.

10. Navigate to **Amazon AWS Cloud** | **Maintain Catalog Items** | **Virtual Machine Items (EC2)** and click on the **EC2 Catalog Items** that you have created to open the form.

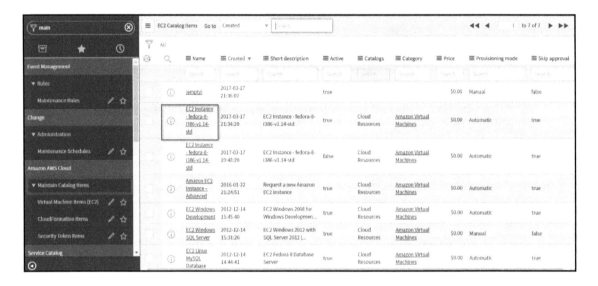

11. You are able to see the filled in information, and you are able to edit any fields that you intend to change. Click on **Try It** to see how the service catalog looks to the end user who is going to use this service catalog. You can also unpublish this service catalog using the **Unpublish** button.

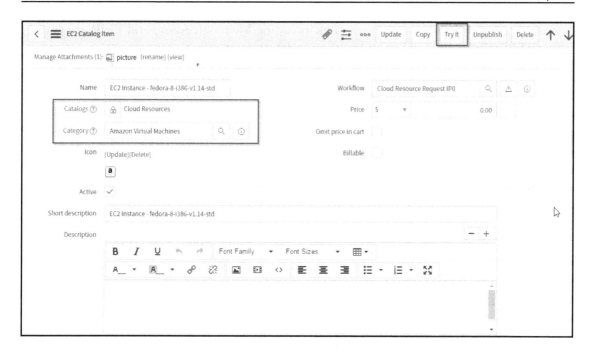

12. We had published our service catalog under **Cloud Resources**, we are able to open the published service catalogs by clicking on **Service Catalog | Catalogs**.

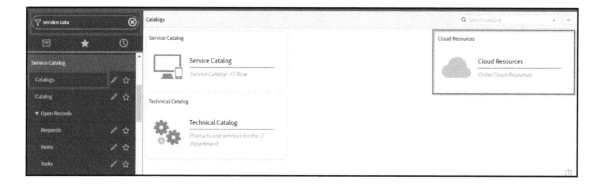

In order to configure other cloud providers including Microsoft Azure and VMWare you will need to activate the plug in and configure the respective fields and options available. Depending on the type of cloud provider you are selecting you will need the appropriate information.

Summary

In this chapter, we had seen how to activate the cloud application, especially focusing on activating the AWS cloud application. We also walked through how to set up the Amazon AWS application and finally we also integrated with the service catalog where people can subscribe for the virtual resources.

6
Automation Using ServiceNow Orchestration

In this chapter, *Automation Using ServiceNow Orchestration*, we will learn about Orchestration capabilities available in the ServiceNow application. We will learn about the Orchestration architecture, setting up Orchestration capabilities and also run through an example before we conclude the chapter.

What is Orchestration?

Imagine school band with all the kids having different musical instruments and playing to play for a song, some kids play drums, some play violin and so on. How does the music teacher make sure the goal is achieved is through tuning the musical instruments that are played by the kids directing them to achieve the required music through the instructions.

ServiceNow Orchestration works in a similar way; there are many different parts involved in getting activities done manually. ServiceNow Orchestration helps to facilitate and bridge the gap by helping to align all pieces involved to automate the required piece of process activity or function. These are achieved through the workflows in the ServiceNow world.

You might have seen or heard about process flows in the real world. Process flows are sets of procedures or activities that are required to be followed based on a set or defined governance framework or standard requirement. These processes are usually translated into the tools to perform these activity. ServiceNow is configured or customized to accommodate defined processes through workflows.

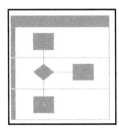

When a process or function or an activity involves an external activity to be automated outside ServiceNow, Orchestration helps to facilitate the automation.

Orchestration prerequisites

The Orchestration plug-in Orchestration (`com.snc.runbook_automation`) must be enabled. This requires a separate subscription to be purchased from ServiceNow. You will need to contact your account representative for more information on the pricing.

Orchestration capabilities

ServiceNow Orchestration can be leveraged to perform simple to complex automation tasks that are not limited the following:

- **Password reset process**: ServiceNow Orchestration can help to perform the password management, integrating with the required active directory or the infrastructure component.
- **Cloud provisioning**
- **Server reboot**
- **Software asset management**

Understanding ServiceNow Orchestration architecture

Management, Instrumentation, and **Discovery Server** (**MID Server**) play a key role in Orchestration activities. ServiceNow, which is on the cloud, talks to the corporate network through the MID Server. The MID Server also helps to facilitate the defined Orchestration activities. Orchestration activities instruct the MID Server to execute Orchestration commands against the target infrastructure component and responses back are sent to the instance.

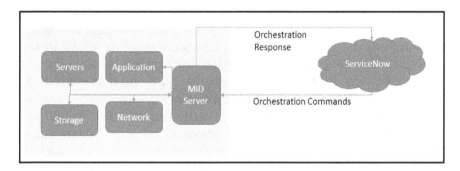

Orchestration workflow

Orchestration is initiated through the Orchestration workflow. The Orchestration workflow launches a probe and puts the workflows into a pause state. The MID Server executes the probe against the target infrastructure device. Once the probe results are retrieved, the workflow is resumed.

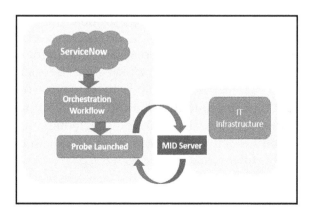

Activities that involve direct web servers do not require the use of Orchestration. Our chapter will be based on the Istanbul release. Let's have a look at the new updates in the release.

 Istanbul release notes from `http://wiki.servicenow.com`.

- Orchestration plug in `com.snc.runbook_automation` now requires a separate subscription; in prior releases these could be activated without separate subscription
- **Credential troubleshooting for activity designer**: A credential debugging feature in the activity designer displays detailed troubleshooting information when an activity cannot authenticate on the target during a test. A tab in the test form displays the target IP address, the credential type, and the details of failed credentials, expressed as a JSON string
- **Software leases for Client Software Distribution (CSD)**: CSD allows users requesting software from the service catalog to define lease start and end dates. Lease end dates are only available for selection if the software is configured for revocation (uninstallation). Users of software deployed by CSD can request a lease extension request, if an end date was defined when the software was ordered. Lease extensions may be subject to approvals
- **Microsoft PowerShell protocol and troubleshooting documentation**: A detailed discussion of the protocols that PowerShell activities use to communicate with Windows hosts is included in the PowerShell activity pack documentation set. Also included are procedures for troubleshooting authentication and access denied errors that prevent PowerShell activities from running commands on a target host.
- **Orchestration runtime plugin**: The Orchestration runtime plugin contains all the Orchestration features required to automate tasks for certain applications without requiring an Orchestration subscription. This plugin provides access to the packs and data tabs in the workflow editor, which gives users access to custom activities for their applications and allows them to reuse data from the databus.
- **System Center Configuration Manager (SCCM) GET activity filter**: A MID Server script filters the payloads from all `GET` activities built with the SCCM provider template and returns only specific attributes for the applications on the SCCM server. This filter reduces the size of the payload, while providing the most desirable application data.

- **ActivityLogger API**: A system property allows activity creators to configure debugging for the preprocessing and postprocessing scripts in activity provider templates. The resulting error messages are displayed in log entries in workflow contexts.
- **MID Server service account for Microsoft PowerShell**: You can force activities built with the PowerShell activity template to use the credentials of the MID Server service. When the MID Server service account is specified, the activity does not try any other credentials and does not allow the use of credential tags.
- **MID Server selection**: Configure a MID Server that Orchestration automatically selects for an activity based on capabilities, the IP addresses of target devices, and the application that the MID Server is allowed to use

Exploring different Orchestration applications: Orchestration and PowerShell probes

Orchestration in ServiceNow extends the workflow editor with extended capabilities that include

- Activity packs
- Activity designer
- Scoped applications
- Databus

There are a number of Orchestration plugins that are available for purchase that include the following:

Orchestration	com.snc.runbook_automation	Plugin to enable Orchestration in ServiceNow
Orchestration - Active directory	com.snc.Orchestration.asset_lease_management	Plugin to provide software lease features
Orchestration - Azure active directory	com.snc.Orchestration.azure.ad	Supports azure active directory management by installing Azure active directory pack
Orchestration - Client software distribution	com.snc.Orchestration.client_sf_distribution	Supports integration with software distribution tools and integration with the service catalogs
Orchestration - Exchange	com.snc.Orchestration.exchange	Helps to manage Microsoft exchange mail by installing the exchange activity pack

Orchestration F5 network management	com.snc.Orchestration.f5	Helps to configure the network elements associated with the F5 load balancer using the F5 network management activity pack
Orchestration - Infoblox DDI activity pack	com.snc.Orchestration.infoblox	Helps to control and automate the administration of window machine and applications by installing the PowerShell activity pack
Orchestration - Probe	com.snc.Orchestration.probe	Helps to run probes by installing the probe activity pack
Orchestration - Runtime	com.snc.runbook_automation.runtime	Enables the applications within ServiceNow to use the data of the Orchestration with the workflow.

The last plugin does not require Orchestration subscription. However, the other plugins do require subscription.

These are some of the key plugins available to install the required activity packs; there are other activity packs available which are not mentioned preceding, including packs for SSH, SFTP file transfer, SCCM, and workday Orchestration.

Orchestration can be used in automating several user cases to automate a process, activity, or function. Some of the automation pieces include:

- Spinning a virtual server
- Integrating with the third party cloud provider and spinning up servers
- The ability to interact with any system web services
- The ability to interact with any password resets, active directory user provisioning

There are even more multiple cases that Orchestration can be leveraged, covering the Orchestration topic in this book we will cover one of the key Orchestration use case which is the password management Orchestration interacting with the active directory .

For us to work on this example, which involves interacting with the active directory, here are the prerequisites:

- You should have subscribed to the **Orchestration**
- Enabled the **Orchestration** plugin
- Enabled the **Active directory** activity pack

Activating the plugin from a developer instance

Follow these steps to activate the Orchestration plugin required to walk through our example.

1. Log on to your instance management.
2. Click on action and then select **Activate plugin**.

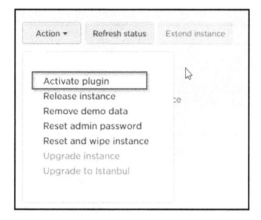

3. Now you will find a list of subscription-required plugins that you can activate.
4. You will need to activate the **Orchestration** plugin and also the **Orchestration - Active directory** plugin.

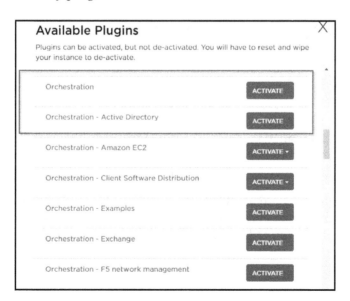

5. Click on **Activate** next to the **Orchestration** plugin. You will see a series of prompts before the plug in gets installed.

Once the plug in installs you will either receive an email, if the installation is taking a long time, or you will receive confirmation on the screen.

 You can also activate the required plug in from the Hi portal, where you have control of the schedule dictating when you want the plugin to be installed.

Active directory Orchestration

In this example we will see how to leverage the active directory activity pack to perform basic Orchestration activities in managing the active directory user management.

Active directory activity pack can orchestrate to management the users and the groups with in the active directory. With the help of this activity pack, the password reset can be managed, and we can also manage the active directory, including creating, updating, resetting, disabling and removing active directory accounts and associated users. In our example, we will walk through how to create a user in the AD.

1. First step: to carry out any Orchestration activities, the MID Server should be ready. In the earlier chapters we have covered on the configurations of the MID Server, and you can follow the steps to install and setup your MID Server.

Search for **workflow** in the application navigator, and then click on the **Workflow Editor** under the application called **Orchestration.**

2. Since the Orchestration extended the workflow with in ServiceNow, you will see, on the left, two tabs which are **Workflow** and **Orchestration.**

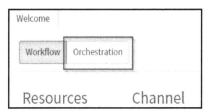

3. Click on **Orchestration.**

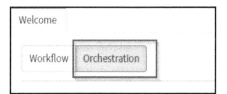

4. On the right panel of the **Workflows** editor you will find different options including the canned activity packs.

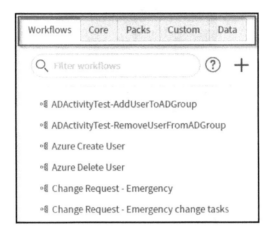

5. Click on the + symbol that is used to create a new workflow; in our example we will go ahead and create a new workflow and leverage the active directory activity pack.

6. A window will pop up in the workflow editor and you will have the option to enter values in the required fields.

7. You will now need to fill in the mandatory fields which is **Name**, and select the **Table**. Go ahead and fill in the following:
    - **Name**: AD interaction
    - **Table**: Global [global] (This is the table you want the workflow to run on, and you select the Global table as you want the workflow to run on all tables)

8. Once you enter the required information, click on the **Submit** button.

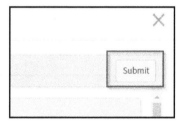

9. After you submit, the workflow editor opens up with the required workflow to be created with the basic steps.

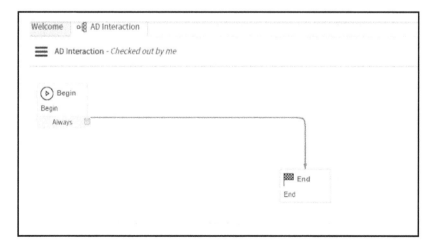

Now click on the icon next to the name of the workflow.

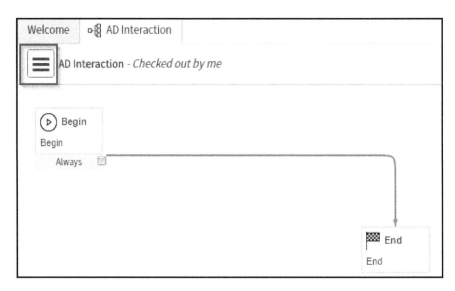

10. Now click on the **Edit Inputs** from the menu.

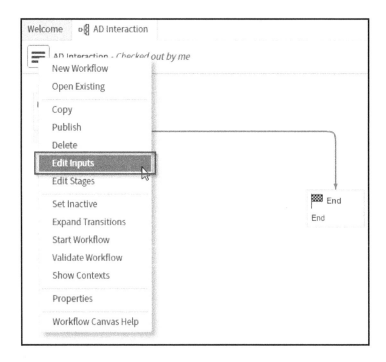

11. Clicking on the **Edit Inputs** will open up a window that will pop up to enter the required variables.

A window appears as follows:

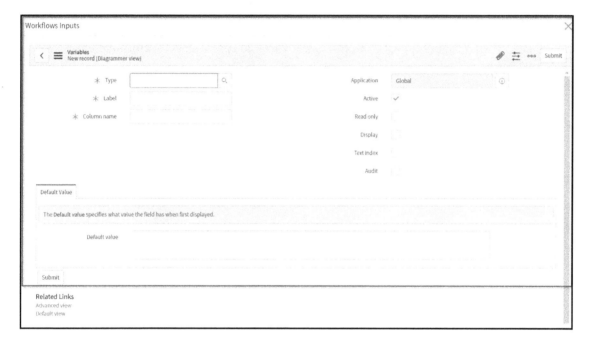

12. Now let's enter the variables; click on the magnifying glass icon next to the type field.

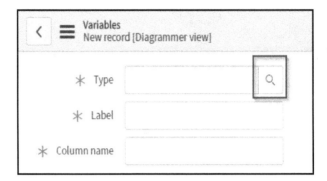

Clicking on the magnifying glass opens up a popup window to open the list of variable types; from the list of variable types, select **Reference** variable.

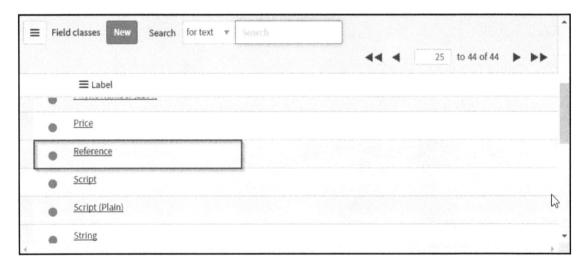

13. Now type in the label and column as in the following; these are examples and you can provide any label you require.
    - **Label:** Name of the User

Usually the column name gets auto populated automatically; the column name can be overridden with what you need it to be.

- **Column name**: `u_name_of_the_user`

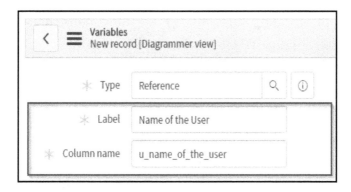

There are additional attributes that can be set for the workflow inputs which are highlighted as following:

14. At the bottom of the window, you will find a tab called **Reference Specification**; click on the **Reference Specification** tab.

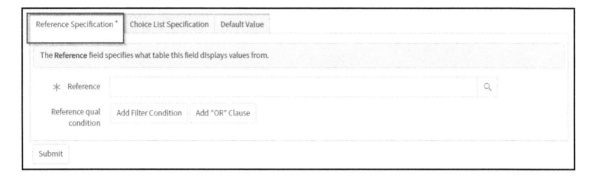

15. Now complete the required mandatory field which is the **Reference** field. Click on the magnifying glass icon next to the **Reference** field.

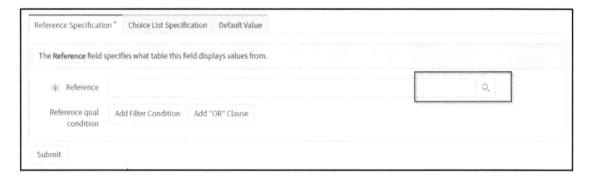

A pop-up window will open up with the list of reference values; select **User** and click **Submit.**

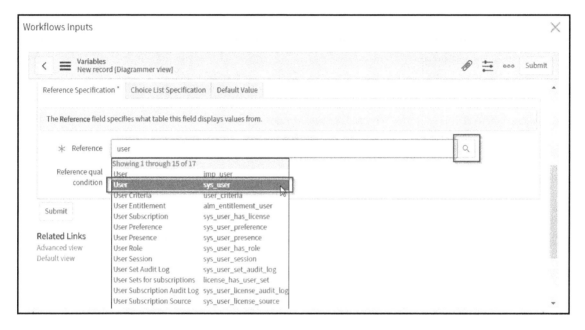

You will get a confirmation after you submit as shown in the following:

16. Next click on the **Custom** tab on the left workflow editor window.

Under the **Custom** tab, click on **Custom Activities** which will expand a list of available custom activity packages.

Under **Custom Activitities** now click on **Active Directory** activity package.

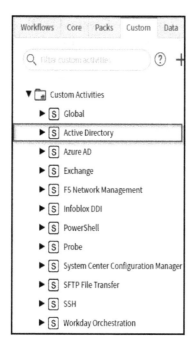

17. Now drag the **Create AD Object** and place it between the beginning and end of the workflow. The **Create AD Object** is needed for the workflow to be able to create an object in the AD.

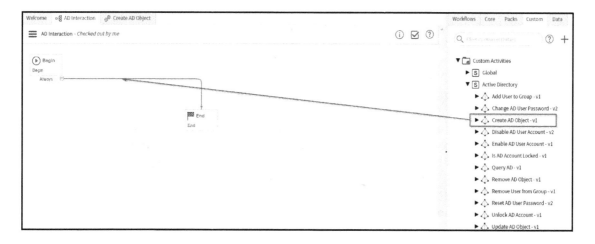

As soon as you drag and drop the **Create AD Object** between **Begin** and **End**, a small pop up window opens up for you to enter the parameters in the required field.

Fill in the required mandatory fields:

- **Name**: You can provide any meaningful name, for example--**Create AD User.**

- **Domain Controller**: You will have this when you do LDAP integration; in this book we will not be covering the LDAP integration side. A domain controller is the one that responds to security authentication requests. Here you will provide the name of the domain controller server. For example--**MYCOMP-GSDV001.university.local**. This is an example of the domain controller name; this domain controller will not work, so you will need to contact your server or the network administrator for the domain controller for testing purposes, and provide the domain controller here.

- **Ou**: Organizational Unit (OU) is a container within the active directory domain which can hold users, groups and computers. You will need to provide the OU where the new user will be created, for example--**Regional**
- **Object name**: These come as an input from the user or the actual user name that needs to be created in the active directory. In our example let's give the object name value as **${workflow.inputs.u_name_of_the_user.user_name}**.
- **Object data**: Here you will need to provide the first name and the last name of the user for whom the active directory account is going to be created. Provide the following in the object data field {**"givenName"** : **"${workflow.inputs.u_user.first_name}"**, **"SN"** : **"${workflow.inputs.u_user.last_name}"** }. The 'givenName' and 'SN' are attribute names in AD.

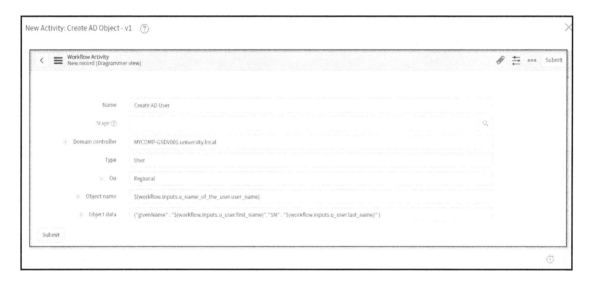

Now click on the **Submit** button to create the new activity.

The newly created activity will appear on the workflow editor.

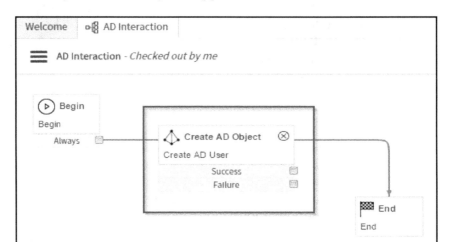

18. Depending on whether the workflow step succeeds or fails, the workflow continues on the success/fail path, and, in our case, we will have them both go to the end state. Now click on the yellow output checkbox of the newly created activity **Create AD User**; then click and drag the yellow checkbox to join with the **End** activity box.

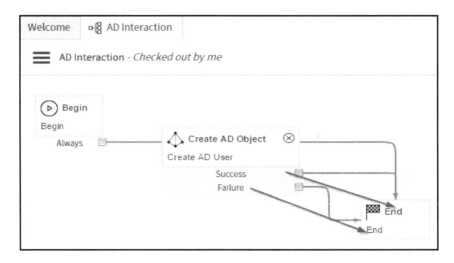

19. Now click on the validate icon to check and correct for any issues with the created workflow. The goal is to check and see if the workflow is executing without any errors.

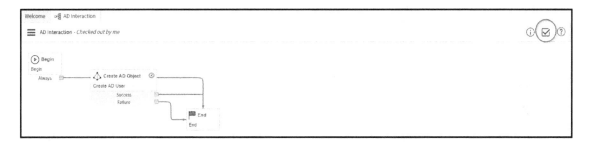

After the workflow is validated you will be able to see all the warnings and issues associated with this workflow.

This shows that you have configured a basic Orchestration workflow to create an active directory user. Its scope can be expanded to check if an active directory user exists before creating the user, and also update the user instead of creating and failing.

Now that we have created the Orchestration workflow, we will need to attach the workflow where required.

Creating a service catalog using Orchestration workflow

Let's see how to create a simple service catalog and attach the newly created Orchestration workflow to create an active directory user.

1. Search and click on **Maintain Items** from the application navigator link.

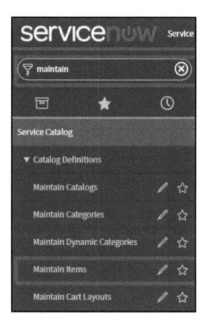

This will open up a list of all the catalog items in the content pane as shown in the following:

2. Click on the **New** button to create a new catalog item.

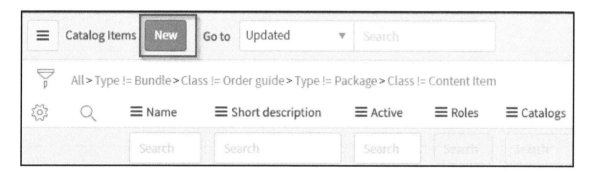

A new catalog form will be created.

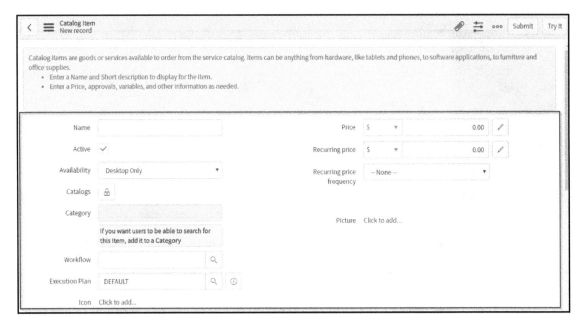

3. Fill in the new catalog item creation form. We can use the following example:
   - **Name**: New user creation
   - **Active**: Checked

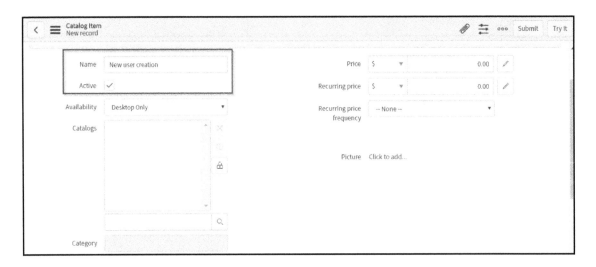

You can enter other information as required. Now let's see how to attach the workflow to the catalog item.

4. On the workflow field, click on the magnifying glass icon.

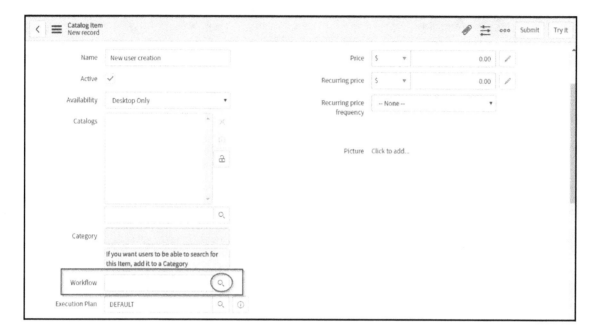

5. Clicking on the magnifying glass will bring up a list of available workflows.

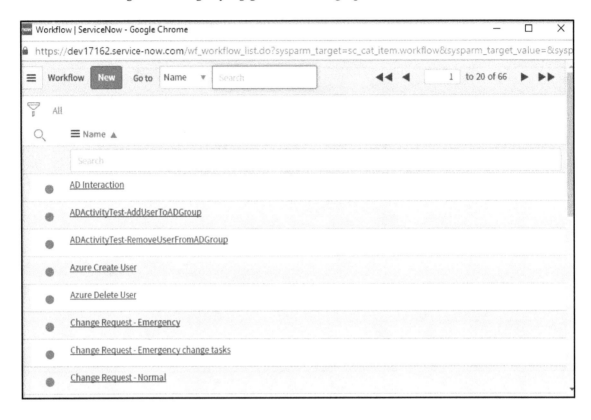

6. Now select the Orchestration workflow that we had newly created called **AD Interaction**.

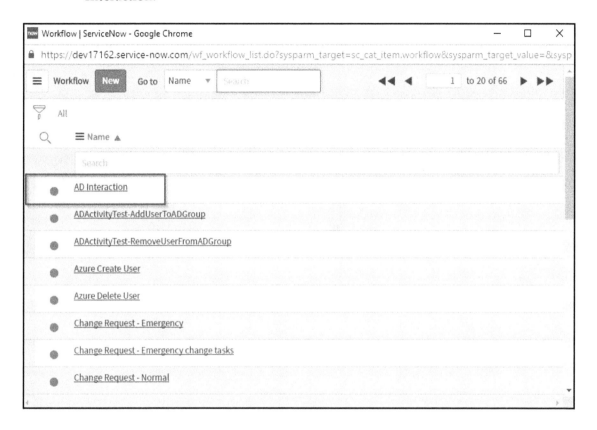

7. By selecting **AD Interaction** you will be able to attach the **AD Interaction** Orchestration workflow to the catalog item.

Now right-click on the header and click**Save.**

You will find different related lists, and a tab called **Variables** will appear. Clicking on **New**, you will be able to create new variables for the catalog item.

8. Now click on the **New** button

Now, lets create three variables to request username, first name and last name from the user.

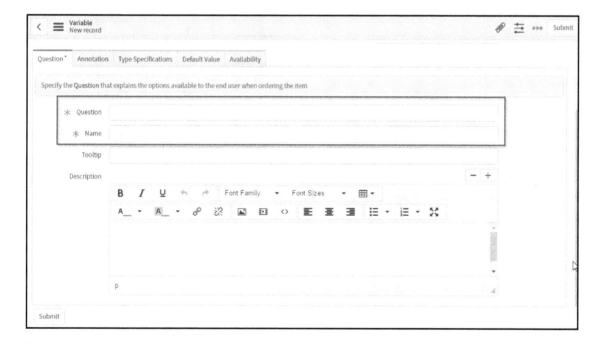

Create the following variables:

- `user_name`
- `first_name`
- `last_name`

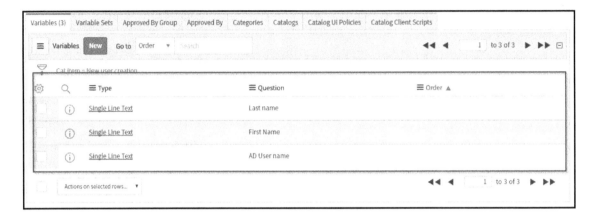

9. Click on the **Try It** button to test the catalog item.

Clicking on the **Try It** button will open up our newly-created catalog called **New user creation**.

10. Enter the values on the form and click on **Order Now** button.

Once you click the **Order Now** button, you will see a confirmation screen with the request number.

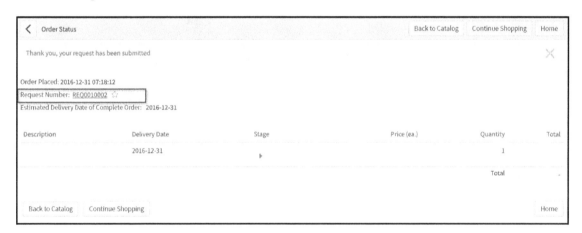

Depending on how you had set the service catalog, the Orchestration flow at this point would have run and created an active directory user, if there was no user already present.

Summary

In this chapter, we learnt about Orchestration: what is Orchestration, Orchestration architecture overview, available plugins, and how to use the Orchestration plugin. We also ran through an example of how to orchestrate an active directory. In our next chapter, we will learn more about setting up and exploring the event management application.

7
Exploring Service Mapping

In this chapter, we will learn about service mapping. Service mapping helps to generate business service maps, which helps us to understand the relationship between the business and other underlying infrastructure components. In this chapter we will learn about:

- **Service mapping architecture**: How the service mapping works
- **Activating service mapping plugin**: Configuring and activating the service mapping plugin
- **How to user service maps**: Using service maps and also changing some parameters
- **Customizing service mapping pattern**: How to change the parameters of service maps on the high level

Service mapping architecture

Imagine a small to large corporation which has a large to small infrastructure where the volume of infrastructure components are huge supported by Cloud solutions, servers, network equipment, storage devices, and so on. It is important for IT to understand the relationship between these infrastructure components that support critical business services. It is important for the business to keep the underlying infrastructure all the time. Image a world where, if any onsite shopping site or a banking website goes down for few minutes, there is a huge loss. So, it is important to understand the impact to business that which IT elements support these components.

Service mapping helps to discover all business service in the organization and create a detailed relationship map of the configuration items and the business services. We have been talking about business services for a while. Let's see what is a business service and see how we create business service maps.

The following are the steps in the process:

1. Create an entry point manually (In Istanbul, we can also import entry points from either a CSV-file or select entry points from already discovered load balancers. These functions are in the **Service Map Planner**).
2. Service mapping checks the configuration item hosting the application is identified.
3. CMDB verification for the discovered configuration items that exist.
4. The host is detected by discovery when No CI record found in CMDB.
5. Discovery places an **External Communication Channel** (**ECC**) request.
6. Use the MID Server to run the probe on the host and discover open ports.
7. Host port information is sent back to ECC queue by MID Server.
8. Discovery receives the host port information from ECC.
9. Discovery creates an entry in the CMDB.
10. Use service mapping to check for the entry created by discovery in the CMDB.
11. Use service mapping to discover the application running on the host.
12. Service mapping creates an application discovery request for the detected host.
13. Service mapping adds an application discovery request to the ECC queue.
14. Use the MID Server to execute the identification sections of the patterns with the matching entry point types.
15. The MID Server discovers a CI if the identification section is fully executed with all required attributed populated.
16. The MID Server runs the connectivity section identifying outgoing connections.
17. The MID Server updates the ECC queue with the information discovered.
18. Service mapping check ECC queue for the information posted by MID Server.
19. Service mapping writes information to CMDB.
20. Service mapping adds the CI to the business service map.
21. Service mapping initiates a discovery request to discover connected CI.
22. Service mapping completes when there are no outbound connections.

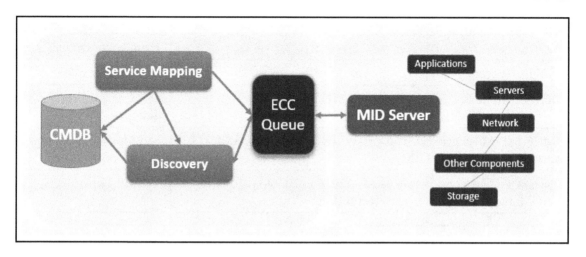

Service mapping supports different operating systems and applications. You will need to customize the discovery pattern to include any other application that the service mapping does not support.

Operating systems supported by service mapping

An operating system that is supported by service mapping means that the platform comes with a pattern for this operating system, but it may require customization to be able to be compatible with your environment.

AIX	HP-UX
Linux	Solaris
Windows	

Applications supported by service mapping

An application that is supported by service mapping means that the platform comes with a pattern for this application, but it may require customization to be able to be compatible with your environment. Common customized patterns are: using customized config-files instead of the default ones, renaming config files instead of using the default name, and using customized tags in config-files instead of using the default tags.

ABAP SAP Central Services (ASCS)	Active Directory Domain Controller
ApacheTomcat / WAR / Web Server	App TNS service
BIG-IP **Global Traffic Manager** (GTM) F5	BIG-IP **Local Traffic Manager** (LTM) F5
BMCCTRL-M Enterprise Manager / CTRL-M GatewayBMC **IT Asset Management** (ITAM)	CA identity manager provisioning server
CiscoACE Command Line Interface (on Cisco CSM) / CallManager / **Global Site Selector** (GSS)	Connect-IT service
CitrixDelivery Controller / Netscaler	DataPower
JRun WAR Inc	EMC Documentum Docbase
FormEngine	Generic application
GlassFish Server	HAProxy
HP service manager application server	HP service manager index
HP service manager knowledge base	IBM J2EE EAR
IBM WebSphereMessage Broker / Application Server / Message Broker Flow / MQ / MQ Queue / Portal	Jboss module
IBMCTRL-M Server / CICS Transaction Gateway CTG / **Customer Information Control System** (CICS) / DB2	RabbitMQ
MicrosoftExchange CAS / Dynamic CRM / BizTalk Orchestration / BizTalk Server / Exchange BackEnd Server / Exchange FrontEnd Server / FAST Search Server / Exchange Hub Transport Server / Exchange mailbox **Internet Information Services** (IIS) / Information Services (IIS) Virtual Directory / **Message Queuing** (MSMQ) / .NET commands / SharePoint / SQL Database / Cluster MGM Node / MySQL Server	Nginx

OracleAdvanced Queue Queue/ Concurrent Server/ Database/ Discoverer Engine/ Discoverer UI/ E-Business Suite/ Form UI/ Fulfillment Server/ HTTP Server/ iAS Web Module/ Metric Client/ Metric Server Net Listener/ OACORE Server/ OAFM Server/ Process Manager/ Report Server/ Tnslsnr Engine/ Tuxedo/ Tuxedo Portal/ WebLogic Module/ WebLogic Server (version 10.3)/ WebLogic On-demand Router/Load Balancer	PostgreSQL Database
SAP BO BOXI ScheduleRouter / Business Objects CMS Server / Central Instance / Central Services (SCS) / **Evaluated Receipt Settlement** (**ERS**) / HANA Database / Java Cluster / NetWeaver Dialog Instance	SuniPlanet Web Server / Directory/ JES
SQLServer Analysis Services (**SSAS**)/ **Server Integration Services** (**SSIS**) Job / Server Integration Services (SSIS)	Sybase
TibcoActiveMatrix BusinessWorks/ ActiveMatrix BusinessWorks Process/ EMS Queue/ **Enterprise Message Service** (**EMS**)	Symantec Enterprise Vault

What is a business service?

Business is the core activity or a purpose forming an organization. There are certain offerings that the business has to offer, and there are multiple components that support the business, including IT. These does not produce a tangible commodity. This is called a **business service**.

For example, a website might be a core business service that is important and supporting a critical business function. These websites are supported by multiple infrastructure components including servers, network components, and so on.
It is important to understand business services for us to be able to proceed with service mapping. Business services are going to be core for service mapping where the service mapping will reference the business service that is defined to

Activating the service mapping plugin

Service mapping is a separate subscription that needs to be purchased and activated by the ServiceNow professional services team.

We have the following plugins that we can activate in Service Mapping:

- Event management
- Service mapping core
- IP-based discovery
- Pattern designer
- Service watch suite commons

We can following the steps give below in order to activate a service mapping plugin:

1. **Activating from high portal**: Follow the steps to activate the service mapping from the high portal.
   1. Click on **Service Catalog**.
   2. Click **Request Plugin Activation** and fill in the request information.
2. **Activate plugin from ServiceNow demo instance**:
   1. Log in to your demo instance and click on **Activate plugin**.

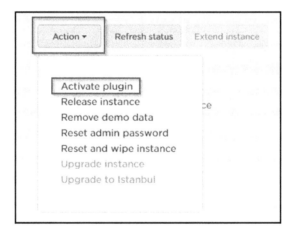

2. Search for the **Service Mapping** plugin and click on **Activate**.

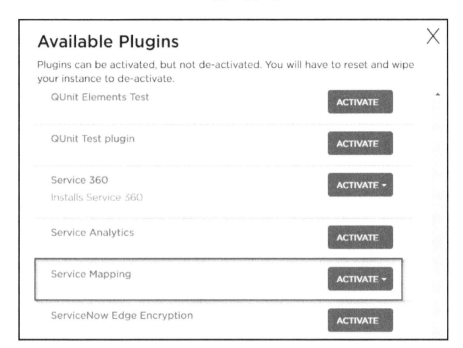

How to use service maps

In this section we will learn more about how to use service maps and getting started.

MID Server setup

MID Servers are located in enterprise private networks; these facilitate communication between different infrastructure components. The number of MID Servers required depends on the size of the infrastructure.

The next step is not make sure we have the MID Server available for our service mapping. That service mapping is putting one more prerequisites on the MID Server, compared to disocvery–service mapping requires .NET Framework 3.5 on the MID Server. Discovery requires .NET framework 4.0, so you will need them both on the MID Servers to be able to run Service Mapping. Follow the steps described in the `Chapter 2`, *MID Server Essentials*, to install and setup the MID Server. To see the list of MID Servers setup. Type `service mapping` on the application navigator . This will list all the MID Servers that are configured and installed. Navigate to **Service Mapping** | **Administration** | **MID Servers** and here you will see all the list of MID Servers that are configured already.

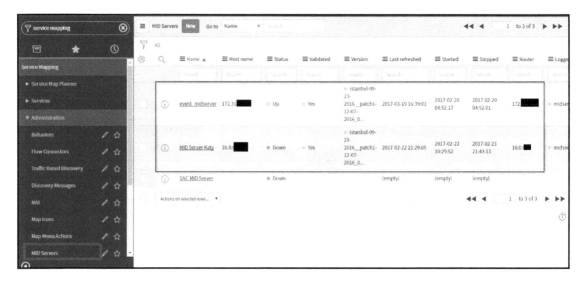

Service mapping credentials

Now we need to make sure the right credentials are setup for the service mapping.

1. To access the credentials, navigate to **Service Mapping** | **Administration** | **Credentials** to bring up list of all the existing credentials. Click on **New** to create a new credential for the service mapping.

2. Clicking on **New**, you will see the list of credential you would like to create, it is the **Applicative Credentials** that are specific to service mapping (The platform credentials you need to discovery as well). The **Applicative Credentials** are the credentials you need to get the permissions you need to map specific application, for example you need specific permissions to IBM WebSphere message queue to be able to map a service including this application. These credentials are used within the pattern.

Depending on your needs, select the right type of credential given following:

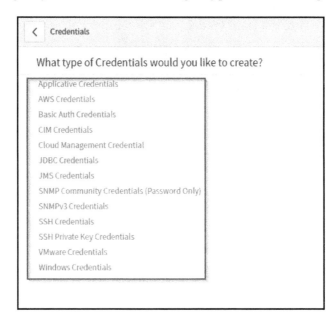

3. Click on **Windows Credentials** and fill in the required information:
   - **Name**: A meaningful name for the credential.
   - **Applies to**: Here you can specify that the credential should be applied to a specific MID Server or all MID Servers. This is important to specify in case you are using multiple MID Servers for multiple purposes. In some cases there might be MID Servers used for event management, discovery and so on.
   - **User name**: Specify the credentials user name and the password.

4. Click on **Update** to save the information. There is a related link **Test credential** to make sure you have given the right credentials.

Business service population

The next step is to start working on creating the business services. Before we start doing that, we need to understand different planning phases we go through to create the business services.

In an organization, there might be huge business services which might need to be consolidated into the ServiceNow environment. Here are the steps that we need to do take:

- Creating empty phases
- Populating the phases
- Creating business service

The important steps are planning, phase population, and creating business service.

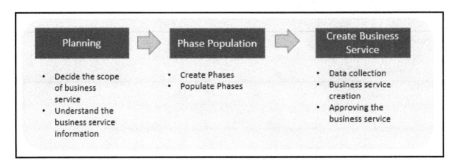

Phases are nothing but groups that the business services can be bucketed into. There are various dimensions that you can group the business services based certain criteria, such as region, by type by business critical, and so on.

Following are the steps to create phases in the service mapping application:

1. From the application navigator type `service mapping` and navigate to **Service Mapping** | **Service Map Planner** | **Phases**.

2. Any existing phases are going to show up on the content pane. If you are going to create a new phase click on **New** button to create a new phase.

3. Clicking on **New** button opens a form; fill in the required information:
   - **Name**: The name of the phase
   - **Description**: A description of the phase
   - **Status**: The status of the phase

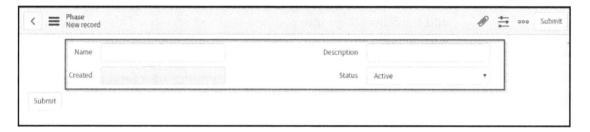

4. Right-click on the header and click on **Save** to bring up additional options on the relation list to create the business service from the created phase. To create a business service from the created phase, follow these steps:
   1. Navigate to the **Business Service Planning** related list tab.
   2. Click on **New** button to create a business service from the scratch.
   3. You also have option to import the business services from a comma separated file that might been prepared already.

5. There are different ways you can create business service:
    1. **Import from CSV**: The information about the business service is captured already in the form of comma separated files. Clicking on **Import from CSV** button you are able to import the created CSV file.
    2. **Import from load balancer** : If there is no business information available, service mapping can extract information from load balancers and transform them into planned business services. This will give you a list of entry points from the load balancers and you can pick the entry points from the list.

6. To create a **New** button, click on **New** button that brings up a form to enter the business service information manually.
    - **Name**: A meaningful name for the business service
    - **Application Owner**: A person who is familiar with mapping the business server and understands the infrastructure and application. This is the person that will get the notification when you hit the send for review button.
    - **Service Deployment Owner**: The person responsible for modifying the business service.

7. Right-click on the header and click **Save**. Once you click **Save** there are additional options available on the related list as shown following.

The application owner needs to test that the service mapping can connect to the devices to make the business service. This step is used to verify if the service mapping is able to connect to the given hosts. Property of a connection is often referred to as entry points. Service mapping starts the mapping from the entry point to check the connectivity of hosts connected to the specified entry points.

When a test is run the service mapping checks the corresponding record in the CMDB_CI for information on credential for the IP address that is specified.

We can create a planned entry point through the following steps:

1. Click on the **New** button.

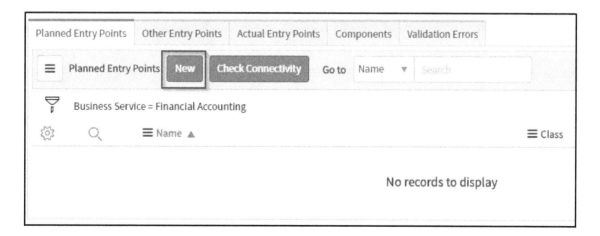

2. Clicking on the **New** button brings up a window to enter the entry point. Fill in the required information for the entry point.
   - **Entry point type**: You have different options to select the type of entry point
   - **URL**: If applicable URL for the entry point
   - **Host Name**: Name of the cost for the entry point

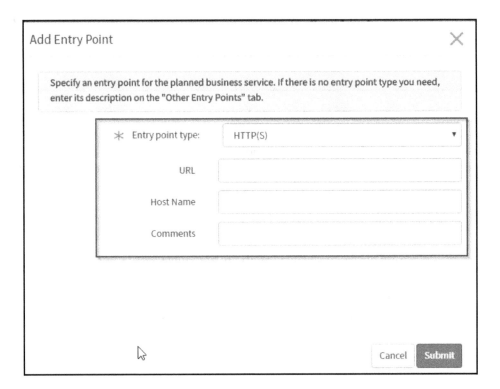

3. In the **Planned Entry Points** you enter the entry points to the service. All entry points you state in this section will be transferred to the **Actual Entry Points** once you have clicked the **Create and Discover** button. In the **Other Entry Points** section you state entry points that may be of interest during the mapping (entry points to the database used maybe). The entry points stated here will not be part of the **Actual Entry Points** once you have clicked the **Create and Discover** button. If there is not an entry point type available, you can click on the tab **Other Entry Points** as shown following:

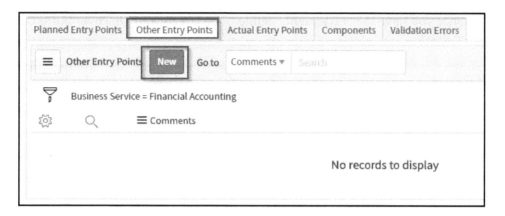

4. Use the **Components** tab to provide more information about the business service. To add a component, click on **New** and fill in required information.

You should add one entry per component and the info about each component. For example, Apache web service version 5, IP `10.10.10.10` listening on port `8080`, and so on. Everything you state here is for reference during the actual mapping, to help you know what components should be part of the service, and to let you know when you hit success with the mapping. It does not have any actual impact on the mapping

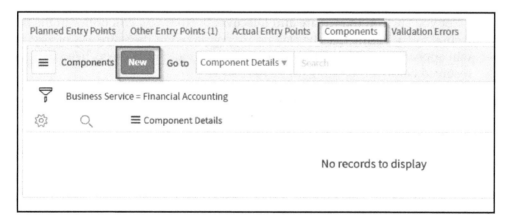

5. Once you have the entry points defined, the **Create and Discover** button is enabled.

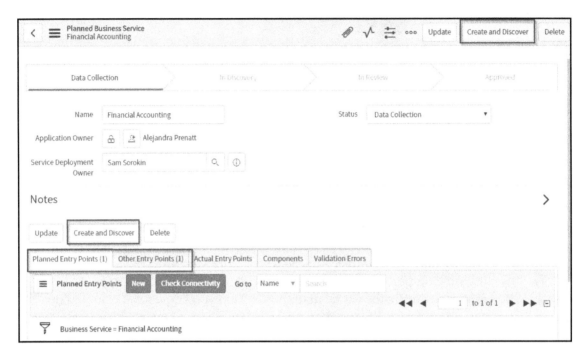

6. After you click on the **Create and Discover** button. You will notice in the tab **Actual Entry Points** that the classes are populated. If there are any errors, they will appear on the **Validation Errors** tab. Any validation errors need to be resolved before proceeding to the next step.

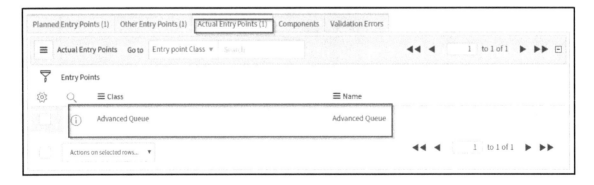

7. A related link called **View Map** appears, where you are able to view the business service map with the starting entry point that was defined. Now the business service is ready to be sent for review.

 Before sending it to review you need to fix any errors shown on the map, and you should compare the findings with what is stated in the **Components** tab. If all components listed in the **Components** tab part of the map, In that case you can send it to review.

8. Click on **Send for Review** button to send the business service and its map for review.

A notification is sent to the the person stated in the **Application Owner** field, stating that they need to review a business service map.

9. Now the business service that is planned is now under **In Review** state. When the map is in review state there is an activity log and notes fields that appears to post any comments. Click on **Approve** button.

10. Once the **Planned Business Service** is approved, the status becomes approved and the life cycle of the planned business service is complete. After it is approved, don't forget to move the status of the business service to **Operational** to make if part of the discovery schedule for the service maps.

Customizing service mapping

In this topic we will see how to customize a an existing service map. To view the business service that we just created and its map, type **service map** from the application navigator, navigate to **Service Mapping | Services | Business Services** to list all the business services. Search for the business service that we just created. There is a column called **View map**, clicking on that we are able to view the business service map

Service mapping traffic based discovery

The traditional method and majority of the data is gathered by service mapping using the patterns.
The patterns are most of the time reading configuration files. There is another method to discover CI using traffic connections between CI's which is termed as **traffic based discovery**.

Traffic based discovery will create all TCP connections that the CI has, regardless if it is part of the business service or not. The configuration base discovery will only capture connections that is part of the service.
Inbound and outbound connections are discovered using the *netstat* and *Isof* protocol and comments. Traffic based discovery can be enabled at different levels

- **Service mapping level**: Traffic based discovery is enabled by default
- **Business service level**: Traffic based discovery can be enabled at a business service level
- **CI level**: Discovery rule can be created to exclude or include a specific CI type for traffic based discovery.

To view the traffic based discovery rules perform the following steps:

1. Navigate to **Service Mapping** | **Administration** | **Traffic Based Discovery**.

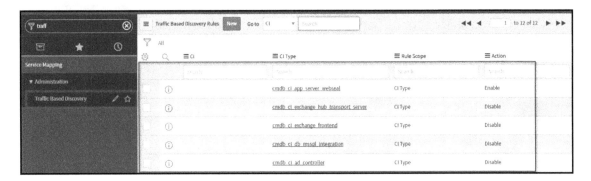

2. Click on the CI name to open the respective traffic based discovery rule.
   - **Rule Scope**: You can provide the scope to **CI Type** or a specific CI

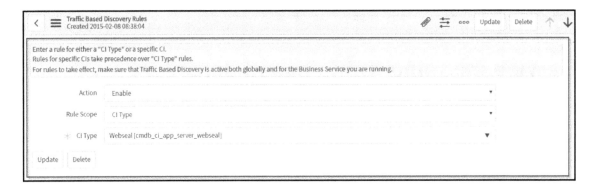

3. The other way to look at the traffic based discovery rule is to navigate to **Service Mapping | Services | Business Services**. A list of business services appears and clicking on **View map** will open the business service map.

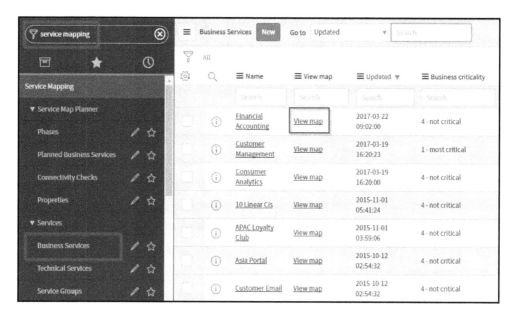

4. Right-click on a specific CI and click on **Show traffic based connections** to list all the traffic based connection pertinent to the selected configuration item

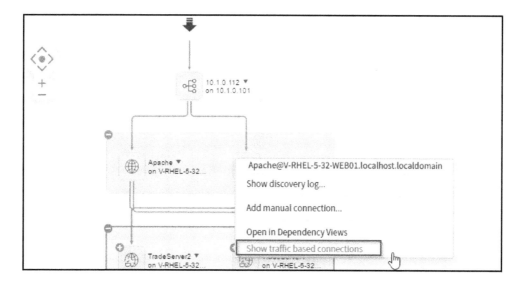

Identifying and fixing issues with service maps

There might be some issues that you might face while setting up the service mapping. It is important that you understand about these errors and you fix this errors.

1. Once again, navigate to **Service Mapping** | **Services** | **Business Services** to list all the business services. Now click on **View map** to open up the map.

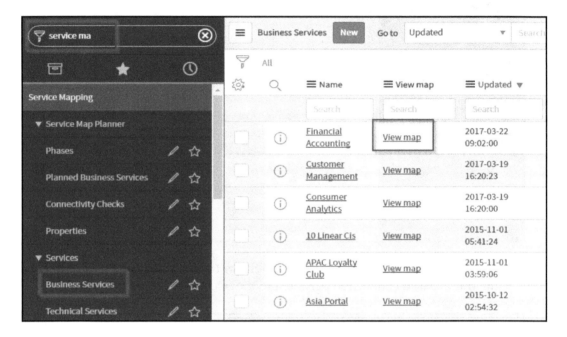

2. Once you open the map you might see a yellow triangle icon.

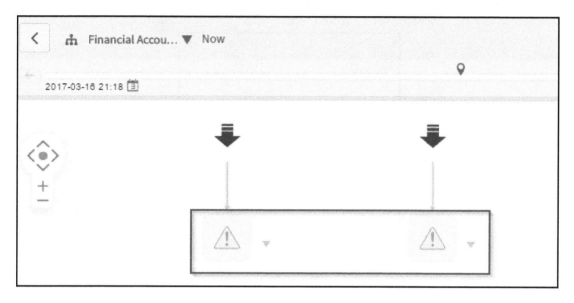

3. Clicking on the yellow icon will display the discovery message to the right and following. The description of the discovery messages are displayed.

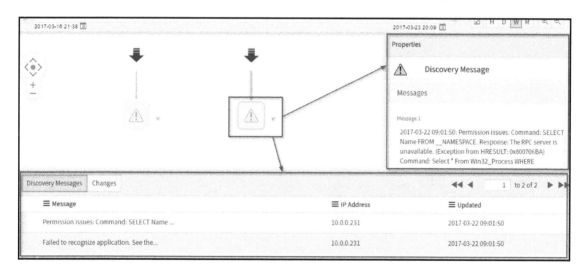

4. Clicking on the **Show discovery log...** will display the errors that are associated with the particular configuration item.

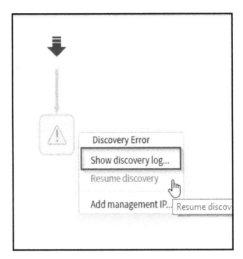

5. Opening up the **Discovery Log** will display the list of errors; depending on the type of error, you will need to review and make the change accordingly and rerun the discovery.

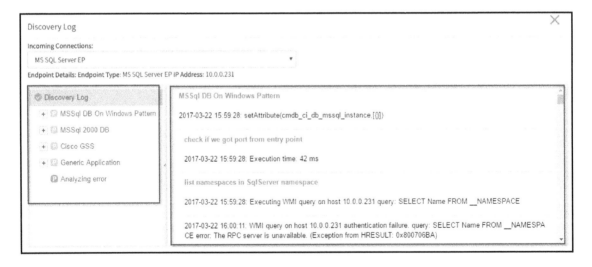

Summary

In this chapter, you have learned about what service mapping is about and we also saw what a business service is. We activated the service mapping plugin and configured service mapping to create business services and create a business service map finally.

In the following chapter, we will learn about event management application that includes, event management architecture, setting up event application, and configuring events and alerts.

8
Monitoring Using Event Management

In this chapter, we will learn about the event management application within ServiceNow. Just imagine the volume of IT infrastructure and the number of data centres and applications used in a large corporation. Each of these applications and individual IT infrastructure components are continuously generating events. These events are being monitored by multiple pieces of event monitoring software. There is a need to bring those events into ServiceNow and generate alerts and also react to the generated alerts to see a holistic view and be able to relate with other ServiceNow applications.

The important thing is to see how the events are effecting the business as you can see what business services are effected by the events, what business services are critical or not so critical, so the operational can decide on what event to start working on first. They want to start fixing the event that is effecting the service that is most business critical and vital, rather than focusing on low priority and low impact incidents

In this chapter, we will see how to setup the event management application to bring in the events from external tools by configuring different options available in ServiceNow event management application, which include:

- Creating event connectors and instances to connect to the external event monitoring tools
- Create event rules, mappings
- Configuring alerts, alerts correlations

Event management overview

Event management is the process that monitors all events that occur through the IT infrastructure. It allows for normal operation and also detects and escalates exception conditions.

An **event** can be defined as any occurrence that has significance for the management of the IT Infrastructure or the delivery of IT service and evaluation of the impact a deviation might cause to the services. Events are typically notifications created by an IT service, **Configuration Item** (**CI**), or monitoring tool.

The ServiceNow event management application helps to identify health issues across the data center on a single management console. Service analytics supports the event management and problem management for **Root Cause Analysis** (**RCA**). It is important to note that ServiceNow event management is not a monitoring tool. It collects events from other monitoring tools.

ServiceNow event management architecture

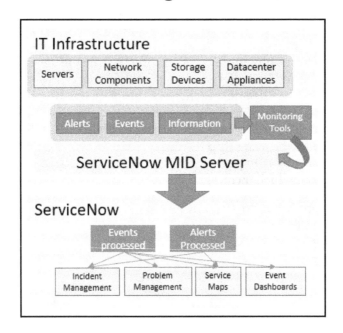

Events, alerts, and information are generated from IT infrastructure continuously, these generated events needs to be addressed appropriately and acted upon. There are several event monitoring tools available in the market to monitor the infrastructure. Event monitoring tools are isolated to the respective tools to handle and take appropriate remediation actions, but these tools are not related to the ServiceNow to be able to:

- Associate the event or alert associated with the CI
- Escalate the events to the right teams

The ServiceNow event management application helps to manage alerts and events that are escalated from different IT infrastructure components or configuration items. Important steps, as described following, are used to configure and set up the event management application.

- **Events**: Events are generated by various infrastructure components and monitoring software
- **Connection definitions/Instances**: Connection to various event monitoring software
- **Event rules**: How to handle the events that are generated
- **Event field mappings**: Mapping values or fields generated by the different event sources and the mapping to the ServiceNow event fields
- **Alert correlation rules**: When to generate alerts and how to consolidate them
- **Alert remediation**: Action that needs to be taken on the alerts generated
- **Dashboards**: Overview of all the alerts generated, users are able to take appropriate remediation actions from the dashboards

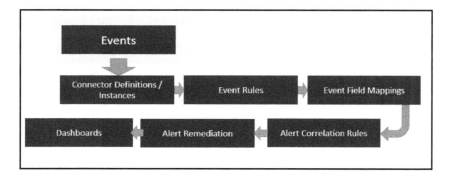

Setting and configuring event management

The event management plugin is available as a separate subscription. You will need to have access to the Hi portal for you to be able to activate the event management plug in. In our example, let's see how to activate the event management plug in from the personal developer instance.

1. On the instance, you will need to click **Action** and click on Activate plugin.

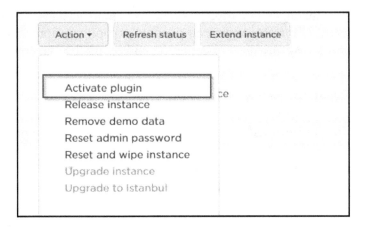

2. A list of plugins will be available which are mostly subscription based. Search for **Event Management** and then click on **Activate**.

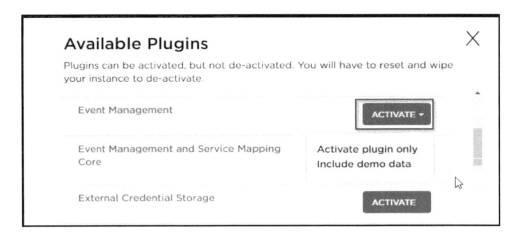

3. You have the choice to **Activate plugin** only or **Include demo data**.

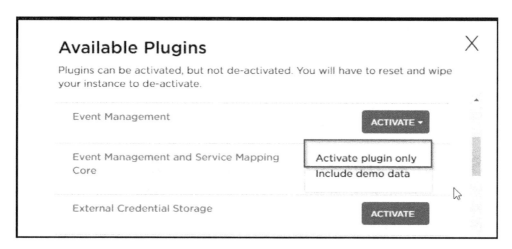

4. You will see the status of the plugin that is being activated. Once activated, you will see a completion message or you will be notified by an email when the plugin has been successfully activated as shown following:

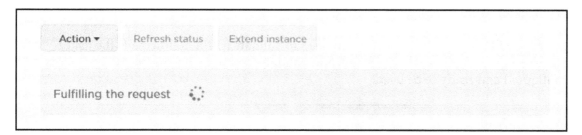

There are two different ways of setting up the event management application.

- The traditional way is manual configuration
- The alternative is guided setup

In this chapter, let's see how to setup event management using the traditional way, manual configuration, and also introduce how to get started on guided setup.

Here are the steps to configure and setup the event management application

- Configure the MID Server
- Set up the event source and properties
- Configure connector definitions

- Configure connector instances
- Configure event field mapping
- Configure event rules
- Configure alert binding
- Configure alert rules
- Configure alert remediation
- Exploring the event dashboard

MID Server setup and configuration

The MID Server is only needed for the event connectors and SNMP traps. You can also use the REST API directly into the `em_event` table, and this does not require a MID Server. You may want to state that, and just say that the REST API way is out of scope for this chapter

The MID Server needs to be installed for you to be able to talk with ServiceNow and the corporate network. If you don't have the MID Server installed, see `Chapter 2`, *MID Server Essentials*, in this book.
The MID Server also needs to be validated for us to be able to configure the event management application.

Once the MID Server is set up, you will need to validate it. The following is the list of MID Servers; a green light next to the status and validated columns means the MID Server is configured and ready to be used.

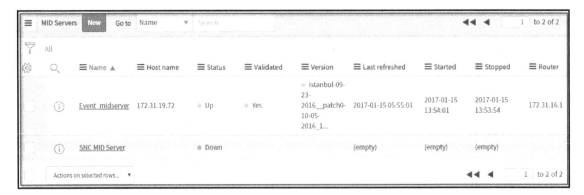

	Name ▲	Host name	Status	Validated	Version	Last refreshed	Started	Stopped	Router
ⓘ	Event_midserver	172.31.19.72	Up	Yes	istanbul-09-23-2016__patch0-10-05-2016_1...	2017-01-15 05:55:01	2017-01-15 13:54:01	2017-01-15 13:53:54	172.31.16.1
ⓘ	SNC MID Server		Down			(empty)	(empty)	(empty)	

Event sources and properties setup

Event sources and properties are settings for the event management applications. To set properties type `properties` on the application navigator. Select **Event Management** | **Settings** | **Properties** to open up a window to enter the properties. Some of the important properties include the following:

- The number of events to handle for event rules processes
- The maximum number of events to be processed by every scheduled job
- Whether multi-node event processing is enabled
- The number of scheduled jobs processing events
- The maximum number of events to be processed by every scheduled job
- Whether alert group support is enabled
- An auto close interval (in hours), within which open alerts will be automatically closed
    - Setting to 0 disables the feature
- Timeout for the impact calculation (in minutes)
- A flap interval (in seconds), within which an alert enters the flapping state. Sometimes the event sources continues to generate events even after the associated alert is closed this is called **flapping**. This causes to fluctuate the status of the reporting resource.
- The maximum number of alerts to show on the dashboard and services bottom panel
- Acknowledge an alert when manually closing it
- Closing alerts will--Resolve incident and close incident

- Reopening alerts will--Create new incident and reopen incident

Connector definition configuration

A connector definition specifies an event source to retrieve events from the defined event source.

The connector definition configuration is only needed if you have an event source vendor that does not have a connector definition out of the box, in which case you also need to create the script to handle the events.

To create a connector definition follow these steps.

1. From the application navigator type `connector definitions` and click on **Connector Definitions** under **Event Management** | **Connectors**.

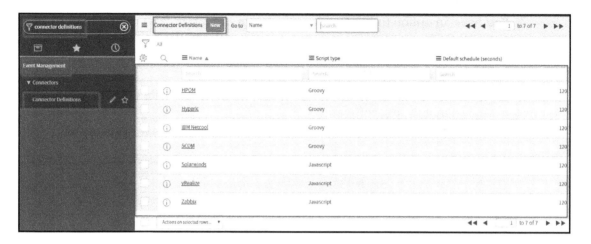

2. Click on **New** to create a new connector definition.

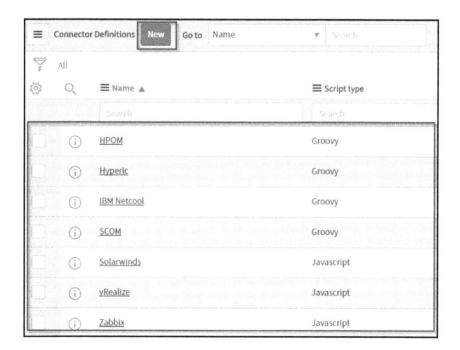

3. You have an option to create a new connector definition. You can fill in the required fields
   - **Name**: The name of the events monitoring software
   - **Script type**: The script type to run
   - **Connector Parameters**: Attributes to communicate with the event monitoring software
   - **MID server capability**: The MID Server to utilize for processing

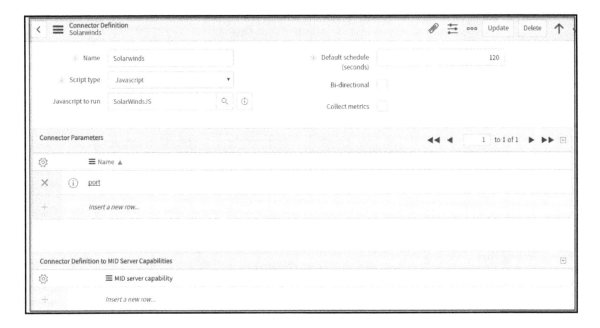

4. Once the credentials and connector definitions are entered, you can click **Submit** to create the connector instance. Alternatively, you can right-click on the header and click **Save**.

Configuring a connector instance

The MID Server gets the instructions through the connector instances to obtain event-related information based on the individual event source. Follow the following steps to configure a connector instance.

1. On the application navigator type, `connector Instances` and then click **Connector Instances** under **Event Management | Connectors**. The list of existing connector instances opens on the left pane.

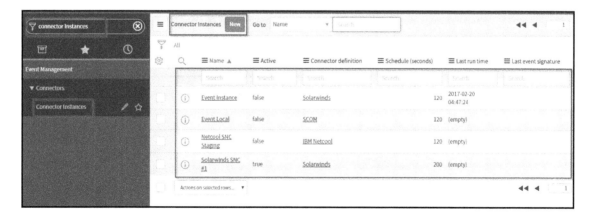

2. Clicking on **New** opens up a form to create a new connector instance. The following mandatory fields need to be filled to create a connector instance:

- **Name**: The name of the connector instance
- **Host IP**: The IP of the event host
- **Credential**: Credentials to logon to the event monitoring tool
- **Connector definition**: The connector type; you can choose whether to select connector definition out of box or create a new connector definition

3. **Credential** and **Connector definition** needs to be configured separately. Let's see how to configure the credential. Click on the magnifying glass next to the **Credential** text box.

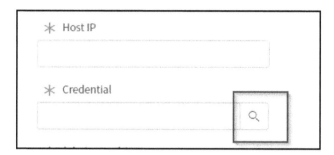

4. Clicking on the magnifying glass bring up the **Credentials** window. You can select any existing credential or click on **New** to create a new credential.

5. Clicking on **New**, you will find different types of credentials to create. You can click on the required credential, which opens up a form to provide the credential depending on the type of credential chosen.

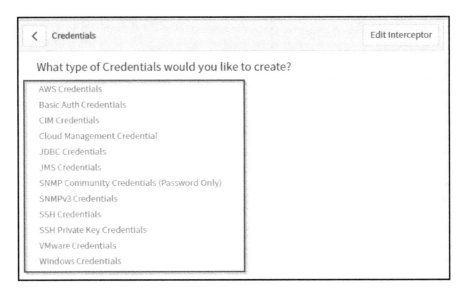

6. Clicking on basic authentication will open up a form like the following:

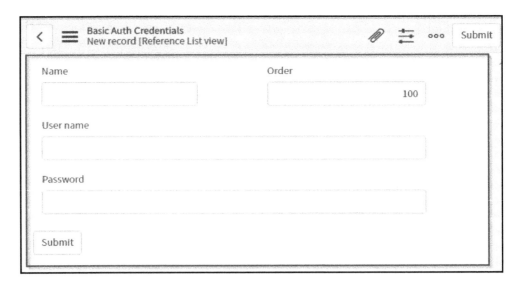

7. Once the connector instance is created you can click on **Test Connector** to validate the connection and credentials.

8. You can see the progress of the connector test as shown following:

Event mapping rules and filters

Event rules are there to generate alerts based on a specific condition that must satisfy before or after an action is taken. For example, similar to your email mail box, you write rules to specific when an email arrives with specific criteria you specific actions to take. Similar to that, event rules specifies the alerts to generate when a specific event rule criteria is met.

To configure event rule, type `event rules` on the application navigator and click on **Event Rules** under **Event Management | Rules**. A list of existing event rules opens on the right pane. By clicking on the **New** button, you can create a new event rule.

When you click on **New** button a new event rule form opens up, where you will need to fill in the required details:

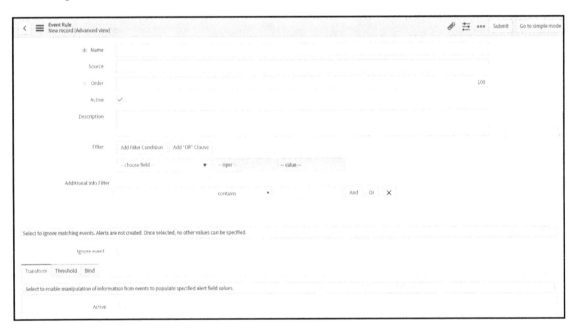

You will need to provide a name for the event rule, then right-click on the header and click on **Save.**

Description of the event fields are as follows:

- **Name**: The name of the event rule, this can be any meaningful name
- **Source**: The event monitoring software that generated the event, such as SolarWinds or SCOM
- **Active**: Make the event rule active or inactive
- **Description**: A description of the event rule mapping
- **Filter** and **Additional Info Filter**: The specific condition used to filter out the event data. The event rule will apply to events that match the filter, which come from the source specified in the form

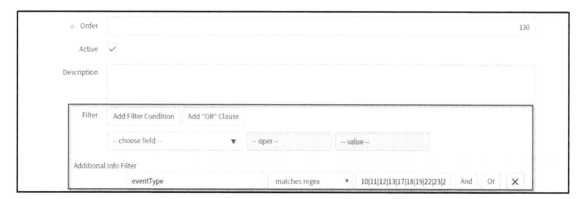

You can configure an event rule to ignore extraneous events and prevent alert generation.

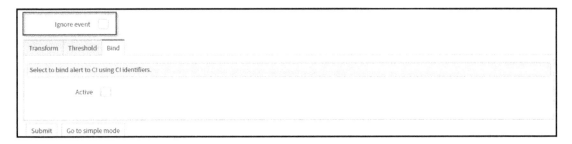

Once the **Ignore event** is clicked the related tabs **Transform**, **Threshold**, and **Blind** gets locked down.

Create a transform to populate specified alert field values as shown following. Using these options, alerts are immediately created from the events. Click on the **Transform** tab and then click on the **Active** checkbox for additional options.

- Clicking on **Active** checkbox will open additional options that include
    - **CI type binding**: If, in the **Bind** section, criteria have not been specified or if the specified bind criteria are not matched, then the legacy binding criteria are considered
    - **Event Match Fields:** Here you create regular expressions to pick the specific fields you need from the event

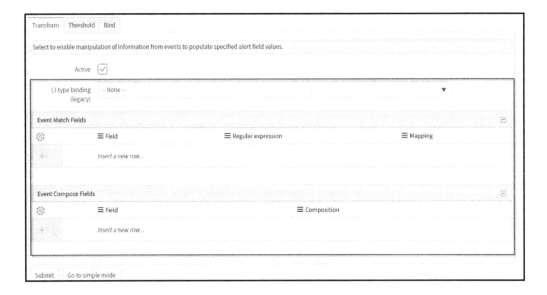

Threshold can be set based on the volume of events received over a certain period. This creates the alert only if the number of incoming events passes a certain threshold. To set a threshold, click on the **Threshold** tab on the related list. Click on **Active** certain fields appear that needs to be filled.

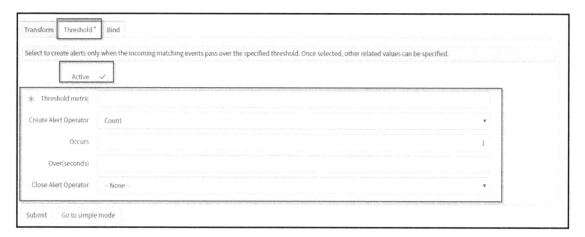

- **Threshold metric**: This can be a logical naming or add on information that is added to an event example--network bandwidth
- **Create Alert Operator**: The math operator which works against the threshold metric and the value. For example, selecting > operator assumes that; if **Threshold metric** network bandwidth is >.

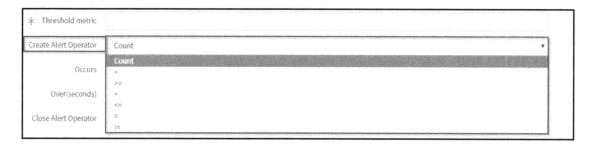

- **Value**: The threshold limit value. This value works with the **Create Alert Operator** and the **Create Alert Operator** works against the **Threshold metric**. For example, if **Threshold metric** network bandwidth is **Create alert Operator** > *:95. Value of *:95 means 95% which means the network bandwidth is greater than 95%.

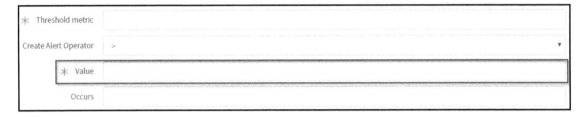

- **Occurs**: The number of times the event needs to occur to generate an alert. This is a numerical value. If you set 5 then the event should occur five times.
- **Over(seconds)**: This works with the **Occurs** field; this is a time bound field which accepts numerical value in seconds. If you provide 60 an alert will be generated if **Threshold metric** occurs **5** times in **60** seconds.
- You can also configure a **Close Alert Operator** similarly by using the filed **Close Alert Operator**.

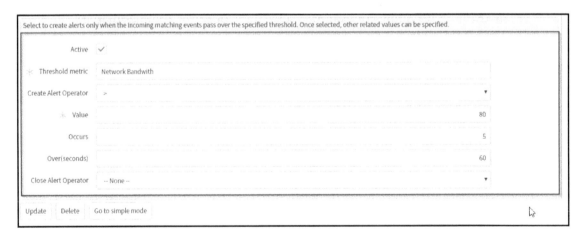

You can bind alerts to a particular CI type. It is important to bind the alerts to be able to associate with a particular CI. For example, if you have an event that is saying that a SQL Server is having CPU over 90%, you would like it to be bind to the SQL server application as well as to the host that is running the SQL.

Click on the **Bind** tab and then click on **Active**. The **CI type** field appears where you will need to select the CI identifier or the CI type to bind the alert to a CI type.

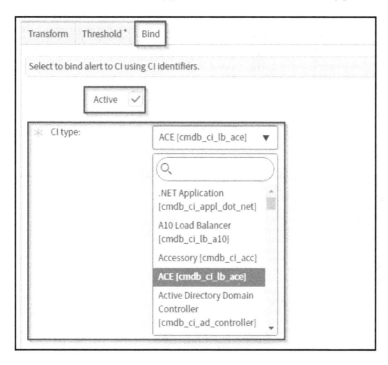

Exploring alert rules, threshold rules and event transform rules

Alerts are generated through events; alerts are setup through event rules. Alerts are nothing but notifications that are generated based on the event rules which require attention. In the earlier topic, we saw how to manage events, now let's see how to create alerts.

Creating event field mappings

When events are generated from different event sources, the incoming event source value might be different than the value in event management application. Event field mapping helps to identify which field from event source maps to which field in ServiceNow table. Once the event rules are executed, the event field mapping occurs and then the alerts are generated. Follow the steps for creating event field mappings.

1. From the application navigator type event field mapping, then click on **Event Field Mapping** under **Event Management | Rules** to list all the existing **Event Field Mappings**.

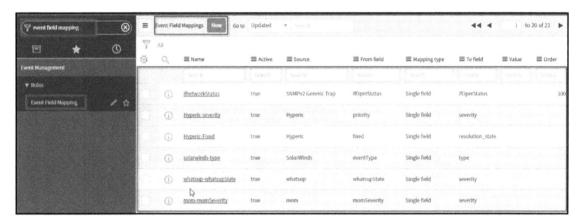

There are default mappings that are provided in the platform for commonly used system monitoring tools, and you only need to create new ones if there are none in the provided list that capture the current mapping.

2. Clicking on the **New** button will open a form to create a new Event Field Mapping. You will need to enter all the required fields on the form.
   - **Name**: The event field mapping name
   - **Source**: The event generating software or the source of the event
   - **Mapping type**: Used to change an event field value. There are different values you select:
     - Single field: Specific values are transformed from one event field to another event field
     - Constant: Transforms a value provided to the new value provided

- **Form field** and **To field**: The event field to replace from an existing value in the **Form field** to a value given in the **To field** field
- **Event Mapping Pairs** : The value that needs to be inserted into the **To Field**

3. Now, right-click on the header and click on **Save** to complete mapping.

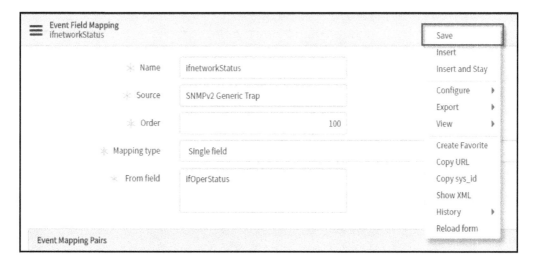

Alert correlation rules

When events are generated and event rules are triggered, alerts are generated. There might be alerts which are related to one another like your service maps, the CI relationship where a parent CI or business services have all the downstream CI mapped below them. Similarly, there might be a parent alert and the underlying alerts might be related to them because the parent alert is generated it is expected that the child alert will get triggered. For example, in a network environment, you have a main router and there are many other sub routers and switches and pieces of network equipment associated to the network. When the main network goes down, it is expected that other network equipment is not going to work.

Alert correlation rules are used for this exact purpose to classify the alerts and create relationships between them. By identifying the primary and secondary, we can identify which alerts to suppress and pay attention to the important alerts.

Based on the CI relationship in the CMDB, a rule is established on primary and secondary alerts. There are different relationships that can be provided that include:

- **None**: Do not create relationship between primary and secondary alert
- **Same CI**: Primary and Secondary alerts need to be related to the same CI
- **Parent to Child**: Alert has a parent child relationship similar to CMDB
- **Child to Parent**: Alert relationship is a child-parent CI relationship similar to the relationship in the CMDB

To create an **Alert Correlation Rules**, type `Correlation` on the application navigator, then click on **Correlation Rules** under **Event Management | Rules**. Clicking on **New** button next to **Alert Correlation Rules** will help to create a new alert correlation rule.

Clicking on configure opens a window to configure **Alert Correlation Rules** and clicking on **New** opens a form to create a new **Alert Correlation Rule.** Some of the important field are as follows:

- **Name**: A meaningful name for the correlation rule. For example: `Storage Limit`
- **Order**: The priority for the rule execution
- **Description**: Rule description

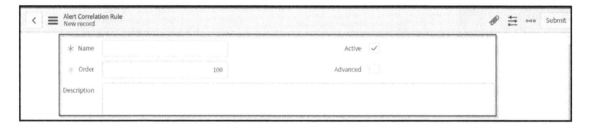

- **Primary Alert**: Filter condition to identify the primary alert
- **Secondary Alert**: Filter condition to identify the secondary alert
- **Relationship Type**: Type of relationship between primary and secondary alert

Once completed right-click on the header of the form and click **Save** to complete the alert correlation rule.

Alert remediation

Generated alerts require remediation, this can be done automatically or manually. Let's see how to remediate alerts manually from the alert console. Search for **alert console** on the application navigator. Click on **Alert Console** under **Event Management** and a list of alerts appear on the right navigation pane.

You can right-click on an alert and click on **Run remediation** option.

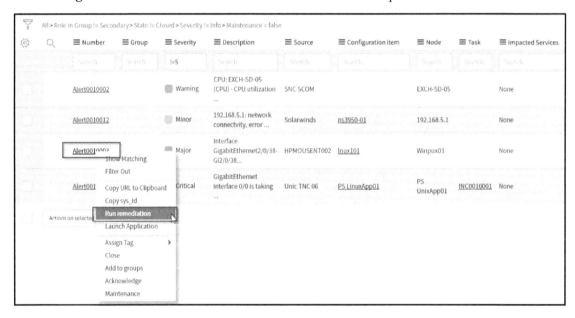

Right-click on the alert that you want to remediate, select the remediation action that needs to be taken and then click on **Run** button.

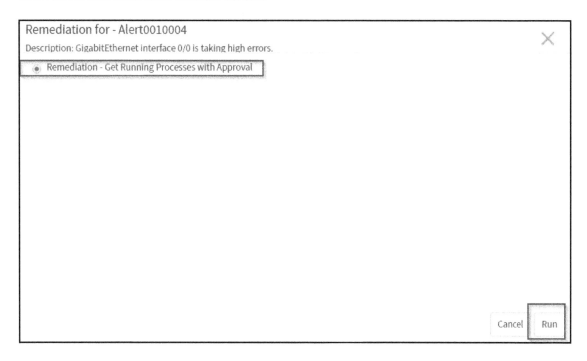

Once you click on **Run** a remediation task will be created based on the defined workflow that is attached to run on the remediation task. A workflow, which can be an orchestration workflow, can be attached to the remediation task.

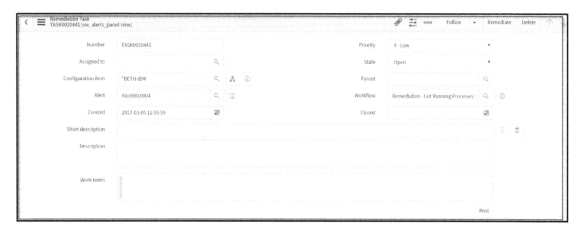

Event management dashboard and overview

Events and alerts can be monitored and appropriate remediation actions can be taken right from the dashboards. You can click on **Overview** or **Dashboard** under event management application. Clicking on **Dashboard** shows the snapshot of the business services that require attention. Overview gives an overall snapshot of the event management application. You can click on the respective alerts to take appropriate remediation action.

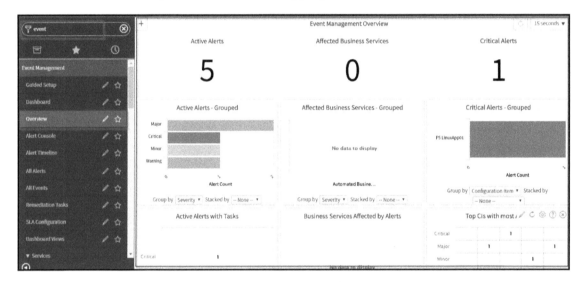

Setting up the event management application with guided setup

We saw how to setup event management application using manual configuration. Now lets see how to configure event management application using guided setup.

1. On the application navigator, search for the **Event Management** application by entering the event keyword.

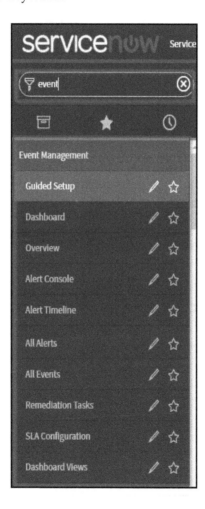

2. Now click on **Guided Setup** under the **Event Management**. A guided setup window will open up on the content pane as shown following:

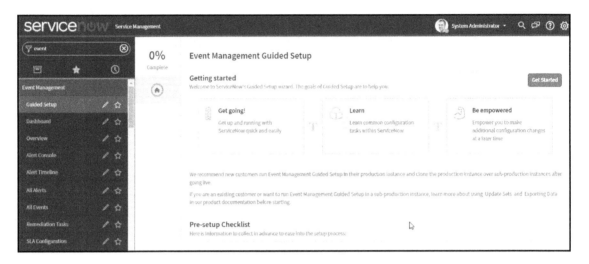

3. Guided setup will list all the prerequisites that are required to setup your event management application.

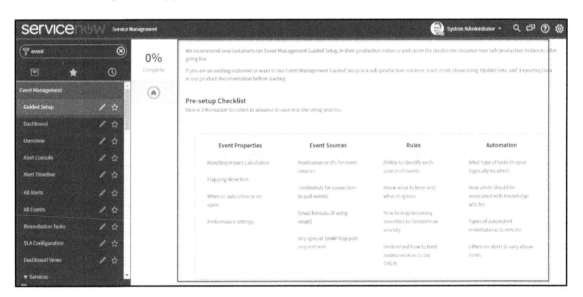

Through the instructions provided you will be able to configure the event management application through the guided setup.

 The guided setup provides a checklist of what need to be configured step by step. These steps overlap with the manual steps that we went through.

Summary

In this chapter, we learnt about event management overview, how to enable event management plugins, how to setup and configure event management application, how to use guided setup, how to create connector definitions and instances, and how to create event rules, event field mappings and correlation rules.

Index

www.ingramcontent.com/pod-product-compliance
Lightning Source LLC
Chambersburg PA
CBHW060534060326
40690CB00017B/3488